The Scott, Foresman PROCOM Series

Series Editors

Roderick P. Hart
University of Texas at Austin

Ronald L. Applbaum
Pan American University

Titles in the PROCOM Series

BETTER WRITING FOR PROFESSIONALS
A Concise Guide
Carol Gelderman

BETWEEN YOU AND ME
The Professional's Guide to Interpersonal Communication
Robert Hopper
In consultation with Lillian Davis

COMMUNICATION STRATEGIES FOR TRIAL ATTORNEYS
K. Phillip Taylor
Raymond W. Buchanan
David U. Strawn

THE CORPORATE MANAGER'S GUIDE TO BETTER COMMUNICATION
W. Charles Redding
In consultation with Michael Z. Sincoff

THE ENGINEER'S GUIDE TO BETTER COMMUNICATION
Richard Arthur
In consultation with Volkmer Reichert

GETTING THE JOB DONE
A Guide to Better Communication for Office Staff
Bonnie Johnson
In consultation with Geri Sherman

THE GUIDE TO BETTER COMMUNICATION IN GOVERNMENT SERVICE
Raymond L. Falcione
In consultation with James G. Dalton

THE MILITARY OFFICER'S GUIDE TO BETTER COMMUNICATION
L. Brooks Hill
In consultation with Major Michael Gallagher

THE NURSE'S GUIDE TO BETTER COMMUNICATION
Robert E. Carlson
In consultation with Margaret Kidwell Udin and Mary Carlson

THE PHYSICIAN'S GUIDE TO BETTER COMMUNICATION
Barbara F. Sharf
In consultation with Dr. Joseph A. Flaherty

THE POLICE OFFICER'S GUIDE TO BETTER COMMUNICATION
Keith V. Erickson
T. Richard Cheatham
In consultation with Frank Dyson

PROFESSIONALLY SPEAKING
A Concise Guide
Robert Doolittle
In consultation with Thomas Towers

For further information, write to

Professional Publishing Group
Scott, Foresman and Company
1900 East Lake Avenue
Glenview, IL 60025

The Corporate Manager's Guide to Better Communication

PROCOM

SERIES EDITORS

Roderick P. Hart
University of Texas at Austin

Ronald L. Applbaum
Pan American University

The Corporate Manager's Guide to Better Communication

W. Charles Redding, Ph.D.
Purdue University

in consultation with
Michael Z. Sincoff
The Mead Corporation

Scott, Foresman and Company Glenview, Illinois
Dallas, Texas   Oakland, New Jersey   Palo Alto, California
Tucker, Georgia   London

ACKNOWLEDGEMENTS

From *Interpersonal Conflict Resolution* by Alan C. Filley, pp. 74–75. Copyright © 1975 Scott, Foresman and Company. From "Attitudes Toward Communication and the Assessment of Rhetorical Sensitivity" by Roderick P. Hart, Robert E. Carlson and William F. Eadie in *Communication Monographs*, Volume 47, March 1980. Reprinted by permission of the Speech Communication Association.   From "The games corporate editors play" by Bill Hunter from *The Ragan Report*, December 31, 1979. Reprinted by permission of Lawrence Ragan Communications, Inc. and the author.   From "Feedback flourishes in sensing sessions" from *IABC News,* May 1979. Reprinted by permission of International Association of Business Communicators.   From "Communication push boosts productivity" from *IABC News,* September 1980. Reprinted by permission of International Association of Business Communicators.   From "Economic productivity efforts span globe" from *IABC News,* February 1981. Reprinted by permission of International Association of Business Communicators.   From "New management styles demand candor" from *IABC News,* March 1981. Reprinted by permission of International Association of Business Communicators.   From "Media packages intensify communication impact" from *IABC News,* March 1981. Reprinted by permission of International Association of Business Communicators.   From "Communication smooths relocation" from *IABC News,* November 1981. Reprinted by permission of International Association of Business Communicators.   From "It's time to put in practice what we already know about communication" by George Muench, Ph.D. in *Journal of Organizational Communication*, No. 3, 1978. Reprinted by permission of International Association of Business Communicators and Eleanor Muench.   From "To Challenge, Wins Worker's Respect" as appeared in *Lafayette* (Indiana) *Journal and Courier*, January 16, 1983. Reprinted by permission of The Associated Press.   From "Don't tell them what they already know" by Janine Ragan from *The Ragan Report,* May 2, 1983. Reprinted by permission of Lawrence Ragan Communications, Inc.   From "Letter to the editor (name withheld)." From *The Ragan Report*, April 20, 1981. Reprinted by permission of Lawrence Ragan Communications, Inc.

Library of Congress Cataloging in Publication Data
Redding, W. Charles (William Charles), 1914-
    The corporate manager's guide to better communication.
    Includes bibliographies and index.
    1. Communication in management. I. Sincoff, Michael Z. II. Title.
HD30.3.R43   1984   658.4′5   83-27099
ISBN 0-673-15564-1

Copyright © 1984 Scott, Foresman and Company.
All Rights Reserved.
Printed in the United States of America.

1 2 3 4 5 6 — MAL — 89 88 87 86 85 84

CONTENTS

FOREWORD *ix*

PREFACE *xi*

CHAPTER 1
The Communicating Manager 1

    Developing Self-Awareness *2*
    Managerial Communication: A Sampling of Real-Life Cases *3*

CHAPTER 2
On The Road to Self-Improvement: The First Step 15

    The Nine-Step Schedule: A Preview *15*
    Implementing The Schedule *19*
    The Schedule: Step 1—Raising Consciousness *21*

CHAPTER 3
Assumptions and Fallacies 24

    The Schedule: Step 2—Identifying Assumptions *24*
    Managerial Communication: Four Fallacies *26*

CHAPTER 4

The Manager's Communication Responsibilities   38

What Do Managers Do When They Manage?   39
The Roles or Purposes of Managerial Work   41
The Scope of Managerial Communication   42
The Two Domains of Managerial Communication   47
The Manager's Corporate Communication Responsibilities   53
How About Loyalty and Productivity?   57

CHAPTER 5

The Hallmarks of Excellence   61

How Many Managers Can Walk on Water?   62
The First Three Hallmarks   63
Can The Average Manager Do Anything About These Basic Attributes?   68
The Manager In Perspective   69
The Fourth Hallmark   71
The Crucial Importance of Management Credibility   75

CHAPTER 6

The Sensitive Communicator   82

Insensitivity   82
Toward an Understanding of Understanding   87
Dimensions of Managerial Sensitivity   88
The Key Attributes of the Sensitive Communicator   92
The Human Dignity Axiom   101

CHAPTER 7

Idealism Confronts Reality   104

Listening To Our Metaphors   105
Myth Versus Reality   106
The Reality of Corporate Politics   108
Dependency and Limited Resources   110

    Taming the Tiger of Corporate Politics   *113*
    Guidelines for Using Advocacy/Persuasion   *119*
    Guidelines for Using Informal Bargaining/Negotiating   *121*
    The Reality of the Manager's Interpersonal Relations   *123*

CHAPTER *8*

The Big Picture: Communication and Human Resources Management   *130*

    Human Resources Management and Risky Communication   *132*
    Beware the Motivation Myth   *133*
    Applying Human Resources Principles to Managerial Communication Systems   *140*

INDEX   *153*

FOREWORD

This volume is part of a series entitled *ProCom* (Professional Communication), which has been created to bring the very latest thinking about human communication to the attention of working professionals. Busy professionals rarely have time for theoretical writings on communication oriented toward general readers, and the books in the ProCom series have been designed to provide the information they need. This volume and the others in the series focus on what communication scholars have learned recently that might prove useful to professionals, how certain principles of interaction can be applied in concrete situations, and what difference the latest thoughts about communication can make in the lives and careers of professionals.

Most professionals want to improve their communication skills in the context of their unique professional callings. They don't want pie-in-the-sky solutions divorced from the reality of their jobs. And, because they are professionals, they typically distrust uninformed advice offered by uninformed advisors, no matter how well intentioned the advice and the advisors might be.

The books in this series have been carefully adapted to the needs and special circumstances of modern professionals. For example, it becomes obvious that the skills needed by a nurse when communicating with the family of a terminally ill patient will differ markedly from those demanded of an attorney when coaxing crucial testimony out of a reluctant witness. Furthermore, analyzing the nurse's or attorney's experiences will hardly help an engineer explain a new bridge's stress fractures to state legislators, a military officer motivate a group of especially dispirited recruits, or a police officer calm a vicious domestic disturbance. All these situations require a special kind of professional with a special kind of professional training. It is ProCom's intention to supplement that training in the area of communication skills.

Each of the authors of the ProCom volumes has extensively taught, written about, and listened to professionals in his or her area. In addition, the books have profited from the services of area consultants—working professionals who have practical experience with the special kinds of communication problems that confront their co-workers. The authors and the area consultants have collaborated to provide solutions to these vexing problems.

We, the editors of the series, believe that ProCom will treat you well. We believe that you will find no theory-for-the-sake-of-theory here. We believe that you will find a sense of expertise. We believe that you will find the content of the ProCom volumes to be specific rather than general, concrete rather than abstract, applied rather than theoretical. We believe that you will find the examples interesting, the information appropriate, and the applications useful. We believe that you will find the ProCom volumes helpful whether you read them on your own or use them in a workshop. We know that ProCom has brought together the most informed authors and the best analysis and advice possible. We ask you to add your own professional goals and practical experiences so that your human communication holds all the warmth that makes it human and all the clarity that makes it communication.

Roderick P. Hart
University of Texas at Austin

Ronald L. Applbaum
Pan American University

PREFACE

This is a book for two kinds of readers: those who are already corporate managers, and those who aspire to become corporate managers. In both cases, the goal is to help managers become better managers by becoming better communicators.

What can a book do? No book can be a substitute for actually practicing, day in and day out, those skills that make it possible for one human being to communicate with other human beings: perceiving, listening, reading, writing, and talking. But mere practice by itself is not enough. After all, bad communicators have learned, through practice, to be bad communicators. What is needed is *guided practice*. Guided practice is practice based upon a clear notion of what you are doing. It is practice informed by an understanding of what constitutes good—and not so good—communication. It is practice, therefore, governed by explicitly formulated objectives.

This book devotes most of its pages to the task of helping you formulate objectives, objectives developed from our current knowledge of what "good managerial communication" means. Hence, it is a guide book, not a treatise. It urges you to undertake a serious program of self-improvement by following a nine-step schedule, with each successive step building upon what you have learned in the preceding steps. It offers you a detailed analysis of six basic "hallmarks of communication excellence," with each hallmark representing an essential component of a manager's communication effectiveness.

The book takes both a broad and a restricted view of managerial communication. Broad in the sense that you will be examining—in the special context of the business firm—all the processes, enumerated earlier, involved in human communication: perceiving, listening, reading, writing, and talking. And restricted in several ways. First, in the compass of a book as brief as this one must be, detailed "how-to-do-it" instructions in the innumerable communication acts required of a typical manager are, of course, not feasible. Thus, for intensive focus upon written communication, you should go to the volume in the ProCom series by Carol Gelderman, *Better Writing for Professionals*. Or for intensive treatment of public speaking, the market is flooded with books on this subject.

Second, although concern for "external" corporate communication is not ignored, space limitations compel us to leave the details of such areas as public relations and advertising to the numerous specialized textbooks dealing with these topics. However, within the scope of "internal" corporate communication, you will discover an enormous range of behavior reflecting the axiom that "no corporate manager can be a better manager than he or she is a communicator."

More specifically, you will see how two different, but interrelated, aspects of managerial communication—the *personal* and the *corporate*—are required to produce the all-round managerial communicator. You will be invited to examine a variety of effective and ineffective communication events in the contexts of real-life cases; and you will be provided with detailed checklists designed to help you improve your effectiveness in such situations as corporate politics, advocacy of controversial proposals, and performance appraisals.

The book assumes that the typical reader already possesses useful knowledge about human communication, and is already a skilled communicator in at least some respects or some settings. (If it were otherwise, we should wonder how the reader could either hold a managerial position, or aspire to hold one.)

At the same time, the book also assumes that the typical reader—being human—falls short of perfection as a managerial communicator. Therefore, the assumption is that you are approaching this book with a feeling—no matter how vague—that you could stand some degree of improvement in the ways you now communicate on the job. (If it were otherwise, why read the book?)

Although it obviously takes more than communication competence to make an effective manager, it remains true that, without communication competence, no manager can reach his or her potential of managerial effectiveness. The principles, techniques, and suggestions incorporated in this book—never to be regarded as magic formulas—should help you to attain that potential.

From among the host of people who have contributed their insights, directly or indirectly, to this book, I must single out several individuals. Rod Hart and Ron Applbaum, Series Editors for ProCom, have, over an agonizingly lengthy period of time, pushed, prodded, supported, advised, questioned, cautioned, and encouraged me. Their detailed, thoughtful, and sophisticated counsel has been indispensable, while at the same time I accept responsibility for any shortcomings readers may identify. Editors at Scott, Foresman have shown themselves to be combinations of hard-nosed taskmasters and empathic helpers. I speak especially of Roger Holloway, Molly Gardiner, and Darcie Sanders. I owe a special debt to Mike Sincoff, my consultant, who has been constantly available as a source of ideas, and especially as a forthright critic bringing to bear his years of experience in the corporate world. Mona Marie Grimsley, who has served as my editorial assistant on an earlier publication, deserves the credit for whatever small measure of success I may have achieved in escaping from the harness of professorial pedantry. I am grateful to the reviewers for their insightful and practical evaluations of the draft manuscript: Thomas R. Banner of Standard Oil of Indiana, and Gary E. Huffman of General Motors. Finally, the book would have been impossible without the unfailing support of my wife Ann, who patiently endured numberless distractions and frustrations.

W. Charles Redding

The Corporate Manager's Guide to Better Communication

CHAPTER 1

The Communicating Manager

We're communicating all the time.

Suppose this chapter were titled "The *Non*communicating Manager." Would that make sense? Of course not. We could never find a flesh-and-blood manager who managed without communicating in some way, with someone, at some time.

So we begin with an obvious proposition: all managers communicate. Until we understand what we mean by *communicate*, however, this assertion is empty. For immediate purposes we shall take the word in an everyday, nontechnical sense, to denote whatever is happening when we (a) send or receive *messages*, and (b) derive some sort of *meaning* from those messages. Messages, in turn, we shall regard as any kind of stimuli—whether seen or heard or felt—that we interpret in a meaningful way.

This is the broad, all-inclusive view of human communication. We could narrow it down by thinking of communication in terms of specific skills: observing, listening, reading, speaking, writing. We could also call to mind numerous kinds of messages, both intentional and unintentional—for example, vocal utterances in conversation or in public speeches, memos, letters, reports, videotaped presentations, instructions, employment interviews, rumors, and so on, almost *ad infinitum*.

For now, enough of definitions. Turning our attention to corporate managers, we all can no doubt think of "successful" managers who were not noted for their outstanding talents as communicators. "Yes, I recall old D. B. He was practically inarticulate. We used to call him the Great

Stone Face. But he sure got results on that bottom line!" But can we be absolutely certain that old D. B. was really an ineffective communicator, just because he was a man of few words? More about this later.

We can no doubt also recall mediocre managers who had the reputation of being "polished speakers" or "verbal wizards." To put the matter plainly: this book will never defend the position that "good" communication automatically guarantees "good" managing, or that "effective" communicators are always "effective" managers. On the other hand, however, the book will be based upon the uncompromising premise that, without adequate communication skills, a manager would find it virtually impossible to manage effectively. In other words, effective communication is a necessary, but never sufficient, condition for effective management. The best managerial communication contributes simultaneously to the welfare of the company, the welfare of its employees, and the welfare of the general public (including clients, customers, suppliers, and similar groups). The kinds of communication recommended in this book reflect in large part the central tenets of what has come to be called, since the mid-1960s, *human resources management*. More about this in the final chapter.

DEVELOPING SELF-AWARENESS

Before allowing yourself to be swayed by anything you might read in later pages, stop here and take a few minutes to respond to a brief self-awareness quiz—the Basic Communication Quiz for Managers (below). By answering the questions you can check up on your current understanding of several fundamental principles of human communication, with special reference to the managerial setting. By considering the reasons why you answered each item the way you did, you can begin to gain insight into your assumptions and attitudes, which in turn influence how you communicate on the job.

Later on, at various points in subsequent pages, the questions and their suggested answers will be discussed, with the emphasis on practical implications for managers. The important thing, before proceeding any further, is to test yourself *now*.

A Basic Communication Quiz for Managers

Instructions: If—on the whole—you agree with the item, draw a circle around **A**. If—on the whole—you disagree with the item, draw a circle around **D**. If you are uncertain, draw a circle around **?**.

A (D)? 1. When Person A communicates successfully with Person B, what has happened is that A has transferred meanings from A's mind to B's mind.

A (D)? 2. Effective communication can be boiled down to two essentials: first, Person A sends a message to Person B; second, Person B receives, understands, and acts upon that message.

A (D)? 3. The ideal all-round communicator is one who (a) is intelligent and well informed; (b) uses language clearly and skillfully; (c) gains and holds the receiver's favorable attention; (d) delivers his or her message in an interesting manner; and (e) achieves the receiver's understanding and acceptance.

A (D)? 4. Communication skills, once mastered, are such that the person who is an effective communicator in one type of managerial situation will *almost* always be an effective communicator in other managerial situations.

A (D)? 5. Generally speaking, the best managers are those who can (a) *initiate* good ideas or decisions and then (b) *sell* them to their colleagues—superiors, peers, or subordinates.

X (A) D ? 6. The most effective managerial communicators are able to take into account a universal law of human nature: People generally resist change. *Self-fulfilling prophecy*

A (D)? 7. If you let employees set their own productivity standards, most of the time they will set standards that are too low in terms of efficiency and profitability for the firm.

Although we shall not be discussing these items until later, you can find out how you scored by referring to the note at the end of this chapter.

MANAGERIAL COMMUNICATION: A SAMPLING OF REAL-LIFE CASES

Before being exposed to specific principles and techniques of managerial communication, consider a set of episodes illustrating some of the numberless ways in which communication pervades the world of the corporate manager. Keep in mind that each case is taken from real life.

The strategy here is frankly inductive. That is, instead of starting out with definitions, categories, principles, or concepts, we begin by looking around and observing various examples of communication in action. The idea is that we will gradually—inductively—arrive at an understanding of what communication is after immersing ourselves in the waters of reality. So, as you read through the case narratives, keep asking yourself: What kinds of managerial communication are being exemplified? To what degree does a particular communication act or event appear to be making things better? or worse? Can I arrive at some tentative conclusions regarding what—in specified circumstances—constitutes good or poor managerial communication?

Most of these cases, along with others to be presented later, will provide illustrative material for topics to be discussed in subsequent chapters. I shall be making, at this time, almost no analytical or evaluative comments. So far as inferences are concerned, you are on your own.

CASE 1 Company A: Manning the Barricades

Company A was a multidivision manufacturer of heavy equipment, with a work force numbering more than 25,000. In the early data-gathering stages of a consulting assignment, I was conducting confidential, in-depth interviews with about thirty managers and executives, located in three different divisions.

One of my first interviews took place in a manager's private office, shortly before lunch. After a few minutes of casual chit-chat, the manager stood up, walked around the desk, then motioned me to follow him over to a large picture window. After pointing out several salient features of the plant layout, my host lowered his voice, moved closer, and gave the "hush" signal. Then he whispered a startling piece of information: "I'm convinced this office is bugged. In a few minutes I'll take you to lunch where we can talk freely."

When we were seated at a secluded table in the executive dining room, the manager pulled a file folder from his brief case. "This," he announced, "is my JIC file—JIC for 'just in case'." He then displayed copies of several memoranda, some addressed to other company managers but others (and these were the most interesting) addressed to himself. It became clear that the JIC file contained documents that could be useful on occasions when the manager might be called upon to defend his words or decisions.

Although I encountered no other managers in Company A who reported a belief that their offices were bugged, I did talk with several who, in less delicate terms, spoke of maintaining CYA files—CYA for "cover your ass." Some managers described the over-all style of corporate management with such phrases as "management by recrimination" or "management by scapegoating." I soon became convinced that Company A existed in a climate of fear, secrecy, and defensiveness, especially at the managerial levels.

It should be noted that almost all of the dozen or so divisions of the company had been experiencing a variety of miseries, including large deficits, over a period of several years. Not surprisingly, Company A was eventually "rescued" by absorption into a sprawling conglomerate.

Managerial Communication: A Sampling of Real-Life Cases 5

As you reflect upon Case 1—and all the succeeding cases—be aware of the "chicken-and-egg" problem. That is, avoid the pitfall of simplistic cause-and-effect thinking. Communication events can be *both* causes and effects. In Company A, for example, which came first—the defensive communication behaviors, or the economic misfortunes evidenced in a heavy flow of red ink? It may be useful to think of a cause-effect *cycle:* certain economic events contribute to a repressive communication climate, which in turn makes the economic problems worse, and so on.[1]

The last few years have witnessed numerous published accounts of quality circles (or quality of work life circles), a device frequently associated with Japanese industries. One of the earliest and most widely publicized experiments with quality circles is the one undertaken in the General Motors plant at Tarrytown, New York, described in the next case.

CASE 2 GM/Tarrytown: Quality Circles

There is no question that, by 1971, Tarrytown was in trouble: high absenteeism, poor product quality, and miserable labor relations. Local UAW officials and plant managers finally found a way to initiate serious, though informal, discussions. Eventually, in 1973, union and corporate management agreed to launch a formal QWL (quality of work life) program throughout the corporation. One central feature consisted of three-day orientation sessions for all employees, in which company and union goals were explained and workers learned the interrelationships among various assembly-line jobs.

But the most important and wide-ranging innovation was the introduction of quality circles. Themes commonly used by company officers to describe their objectives were *"face-to-face communication between management and employees,"* and *"industrial democracy"* (IABC News, 1981, p. 1; emphasis added.) A published description of the procedures tells us that quality circles at Tarrytown involve small groups of employees meeting on a regular basis "to discuss solutions to job-related problems and establish timetables for implementing those solutions." Each quality circle includes "a leader, usually a foreman or supervisor," as well as a "facilitator, who assigns responsibilities within the group" (IABC News, 1981, p. 1).

Evaluations of the results of the Tarrytown QWL program have been uniformly favorable, almost extravagantly so. It has been "credited not only with boosting productivity, but also with saving the plant from possible closure" (IABC News, 1981, p. 1). And Ray Calore, a UAW official,

---

[1] For those interested in pursuing the matter, this is an example of what communication scholars have called the *punctuation problem.* In a chain of events, how do we determine the starting point? Who, for instance, said what to whom and thus "started" a bitter quarrel between husband and wife? A classic discussion of the punctuation problem can be found in Watzlawick, Beavin, and Jackson, 1967.

has testified that the plant is "no longer involved in the adversary rat race" (Business Week, 1980, p. 101).
Sources: Business Week, June 30, 1980, p. 101; IABC News, February 1981, p. 1 (published by the International Association of Business Communicators).

Although this is not the place to review debates about quality circles, we should keep in mind that, despite torrents of praise, quality circles have been attacked by thoughtful critics. Some, for example, have charged that quality circles have been used as a device for squelching employee complaints or disarming militant unionism (Lewin, 1981; Nadler & Lawler, 1983; Parker & Hansen, 1983). But even the critics concede that quality circles need not be tools serving devious ends. We must acknowledge the unhappy fact that just about any communication technique is vulnerable to subversion in the hands of ingenious charlatans. In the present context, the main point to note is that a quality circle is a communication technique.

In Case 3 we examine a ubiquitous organizational problem: the erecting of barriers to "protect" higher management from upward-directed messages.

CASE 3 Company B: The Management Maze

Company B—like all too many business firms—was insensitive to the importance of upward communication. Not only the rank-and-file employees but members of lower and middle management found it difficult to penetrate the maze of staff echelons surrounding the senior executives at corporate headquarters. The experience, then, of one middle manager is not surprising. This manager, an unusually good listener, became convinced that almost all employees were in favor of a more flexible work schedule for the summer months: longer hours Mondays through Thursdays, with Friday afternoons off. But he had to conduct a campaign lasting many months before he could get the word up to the CEO. Ironically, when he did get the message, the CEO enthusiastically endorsed the proposal—which has been acclaimed as a brilliant innovation.

A somewhat different atmosphere existed in Company C, described in Case 4.

CASE 4 Company C: Open Lines

Company C is a high-tech manufacturer of complex equipment, and its sole customer is the U.S. Department of Defense. At the plant where this episode took place, management subscribed to a vigorous and comprehensive policy of opening up all the lines of communication, of listening carefully to the rank and file, and especially of being completely honest in handling bad news.

On this particular occasion, top management, in consultation with people in the personnel department, had issued a written proclamation ordering a radical change in the vacation schedules for various classifications of employees. Almost overnight, a storm of protest burst forth. Within a few days, management realized that—contrary to its own much-heralded philosophy of listening and consulting—it had plunged ahead without benefit of employee input, resulting in a wrong-headed decision.

So what did management do? Take up defensive positions behind a barricade of rationalizations? Not at all. The plant manager did something that is almost unheard of in any organization: he admitted that he had made a serious mistake! On bulletin boards throughout the plant, workers could read on a large poster an oversize heading proclaiming "WE GOOFED!" (A short time later, management-employee conferences produced a greatly revised vacation schedule that apparently satisfied all parties.)

Source: The author, as consultant.

The next case involves a massive communication effort developed to alleviate the sticky mess that almost inevitably confronts any company when it relocates its base of operations.

CASE 5 AT&T Long Lines: Moving and Communicating

In 1980, AT&T Long Lines relocated from Washington, D.C., to Oakton, Virginia—a distance of twenty-three miles. The company's communication staff people were given two years of lead time to develop an employee communication program designed to help make the move as easy as possible for everyone. The earliest announcement of the move was issued in a bulletin in January 1978. "But," said Michael Zeaman, manager of public relations, "there had been lots of rumors, and people were starting to ask questions, ranging from the nature of the new building to such matters as transportation and mail delivery."

One of the first steps in the communication program was the establishment of a "questioning process with face-to-face meetings between managers and employees, and in-office question boxes." Nearly six hundred questions came in from employees. The main vehicle for answering these questions was an eight-page newsletter, the *Oakton Update*. This newsletter appeared as often as twice a month by January 1980 (six months before the move). Copies went not only to employees but to 350 business leaders in the area.

A handbook, *Oakton in a Nutshell*, was distributed to employees two weeks before the move. It was "part of a 'First Day Kit' that also included such useful odds and ends as road maps, change of address cards, transit schedules and auto registration cards." Other techniques and materials included exhibits and slide shows (one exhibit was located in a shopping center); bus tours of the new building; meetings in which transit representatives explained bus routes from Washington to Oakton; videotapes; a pamphlet, *Building for the Future Today*, focusing upon innovative features in the new facility; and "open house tours of the new building for employees, shareholders and community members." Zeaman reported that

about 99 percent of all employees made the move to Oakton, but the company also helped some to find new jobs in other AT&T divisions or with other employers in the area.
Source: "Communication Smooths Relocation," *IABC News,* November 1981, p. 4 (published by the International Association of Business Communicators).

Whereas management in AT&T Long Lines carried out a policy of full information disclosure, the management of Company D (Case 6) presents a starkly different picture.

CASE 6 Company D: Executive Paranoia

The executives in Company D were described by a man who had formerly served as editor of corporate publications, not only for Company D but for several other large and well-known U.S. firms. According to this editor, top management was characteristically afraid to release information to employees; executives were a bit on the paranoid side, suspicious that employees would misinterpret every word they uttered.

This paranoia reached the point of fear to announce even good news. Management particularly avoided use of such a frank and simple word as *bonus.* Hence, every time the company saw fit to grant its employees "an across-the-board increase, it announced a 'general salary adjustment,' which always sounded to me as if it might be downward rather than upward."

Several of the top managers wanted the editor to follow a policy of "If it won't sell, don't run it." This rule was cited by a manager who objected to running a story "that recognized a worker's benevolent efforts outside the company." As the editor later remarked, "Who knows how much better a sales job that employee might have done if he'd seen his extracurricular activities published in the company newspaper?"
Source: Bill Hunter, "The Games Corporate Editors Play," *Ragan Report,* December 31, 1979.

An example of the impact a manager's egocentricity may exert upon a mass audience confronts us in Case 7.

CASE 7 Company E: Making the Boss Look Good

Again we have the testimony of a corporate editor: "The objectives of our employee publication are ideal: to inform, to explain, to educate, to be honest, to reward. . . . The reality, however, boils down to this: Our publication exists to make our president look good to his boss in corporate headquarters. This objective is not written anywhere; it's never been verbalized; but it's quickly understood. 'If you want your stories approved, make Mr. H. look good.'"
Source: Letter to the editor, *Ragan Report,* April 20, 1981.

We should bear in mind the possibility that Mr. H in Case 7 is the victim of a corporate climate largely created by his "boss in corporate headquarters" and that he is utilizing every available means of self-preservation. Throughout this book we shall see demonstrations of the rule that a person's motives and feelings (especially when fear and defensiveness are involved) are powerful determinants of the way that person communicates.

This rule is highly relevant to what happens in Case 8. In this instance, two top executives, despite a cordial friendship going back over the years, work themselves into a spider's web of communication traps.

CASE 8 Company F: The President and the Personnel Manager

Company F is a small high-tech firm (150 employees) owned by the president and his family. It manufactures a component of delicate complexity that performs a crucial function in a sophisticated measuring instrument. The personnel manager (hereinafter referred to as the PM) was, at the time our narrative begins, the only woman holding a supervisory or managerial position in the company. She had been with the company for many years, and she and her husband had been close personal friends of the president and his wife.

However, for about the last two years the PM and the president had found themselves drifting apart. Their socializing off the job had virtually ended, and job-related conferences between the two of them—formerly a frequent occurrence—had become a rare event. This state of affairs appeared to have begun at about the time the president, after prolonged soul-searching and consultation of contemporary management literature, had decided to effect a drastic change in management philosophy. With the active intervention of an academic counselor, the president had made strenuous efforts to convert the company from a paternalistic to a participative managerial style, extending to all levels of supervisors and employees. A central device for inducing this change was a program of high-level management conferences. These meetings, conducted by the president with the academic consultant always present as a dominant contributor, were both frequent and lengthy. The basic theme was an effort to apply McGregor's famous Theory Y view of management.

During all this time the PM felt more and more alienated, in fact almost isolated, from the president and the other managers. No longer was the president available for the cozy and frank conversations the two of them had enjoyed for years. On many occasions, according to her testimony, the PM felt like an outsider at management meetings. The other participants would spring "surprises" upon her and (allegedly) put her down as an old fogy ignorant of the latest management thinking. At the same time, however, it was her obligation as personnel manager to administer the old policies, since they were still incorporated in the company "bible"—the employees' manual. In short, the PM perceived herself as occupying an impossible role, caught between conflicting demands and subjected to confusing or contradictory messages from the president.

At the joint request of both the president and the PM, and with the consent of the academic consultant already involved, I was asked to serve as a second consultant on a short-term basis. My assignment was (fortunately) not to produce a magic cure, but to act as a catalyst. If possible, I was to assist the president and the PM in finding ways to reestablish "open" communication. One important technique designed to help them achieve this objective was having them exchange detailed written documents setting forth with complete candor their *perceptions* of all the factors leading up to the present difficulty.

A perusal of these documents quickly confirmed that wide divergences existed between the perceptions of the president and the PM. Indeed, this gap was so wide that an outside observer would have supposed that the two persons were describing two different company situations. Whose perceptions were "correct"? I cannot answer this question. In fact, it may be the wrong question. All that matters is that reality was different for each of the two. The crucial requirement was that somehow each of these well-meaning individuals could be brought to the point, not necessarily of accepting the perceptions of the other, but of appreciating how those perceptions came about.

No such understanding could ever be attained unless each party *communicated* to the other party exactly how he or she felt, and why. Brutal honesty was essential. This "criss-cross" comparison of perceptions, understandably, was a nerve-wracking experience for both the president and the PM. Because of the high level of emotional involvement, candid communication between the two would probably have been impossible without the safety-valve function of the third-party consultant.

To convey some feeling for the kind of communication that had to take place if real understanding was to develop, I present below a few excerpts from the document written by the PM. Keep in mind that these represent only *her* perceptions; for the most part, the president's perceptions were different. Aside from minor changes to enhance clarity and maintain confidentiality, these are the words of the original document.

During the time when we've *both* been working towards a participatory method of management, we have been saddled with an authoritarian Policy Manual—one that dictates that the Personnel Manager has many requirements and responsibilities—in conflict with participatory management. A manual that *I* have had to administer until it can be replaced. This has created a credibility gap for me.

Since I was administering things, and still making a lot of authoritarian decisions as decreed by the Policy Manual, I was perceived as "inflexible." It's been a long and difficult experience for me, with no recognized structure for determining who makes which inputs.

Perhaps I was wrong in declining the opportunity to attend those meetings with you. . . . But at the time I was trying to be sensitive to your efforts to establish a new role of leadership for yourself.

Uncertainty and ambiguity concerning my role were a problem for me. Sometimes I was only a sounding board, but at other times I was providing the inputs and making specific recommendations. I felt that the resolution of *top-level* people-relations problems were beyond my expertise. . . . How do I keep communication lines "open" without becoming a tattle-tale in the middle (right now I'm the one both sides are talking to)?
I resented having my research, my ideas . . . filtered through someone else to you, when I used to work directly with you before. I now perceive conflict in almost every aspect of those working relationships—generated, no doubt, by the total *system* as much as by any *individuals.*

After several private conferences, the president and the PM were able to reduce the level of tension and misunderstanding between them. However, they also came to a mutual decision that the PM's credibility and over-all effectiveness had been so severely damaged that the best long-term solution for all parties was that the PM should resign. This she did.

The next two cases present examples of communication campaigns especially mounted to combat serious organizational difficulties. According to the news accounts, both efforts were highly successful.

CASE 9 Company G: Safety Rules

Company G is described as having come through "a period of rapid growth where the primary concern was getting the product out the door." However, there came a time when management perceived a serious problem: safety regulations were being flagrantly violated, with a dramatic rise in the accident rate. Staff members specializing in employee communication were called in to help devise a program to induce employees to use safety equipment and to make clear that management was sincerely interested in the well-being of its employees. The result was a "communication package" consisting of a variety of techniques, materials, and events. Some of the components were a leader's guide for supervisors to be used in conducting employee discussion meetings, a videotape demonstrating "managers, union leaders and employees working together," brochures for use in the discussion, and a "follow-up reward program." Results: "compliance with safety rules . . . rose from 42% to 99% in one week."
Source: *IABC News,* March 1981, p. 11 (published by the International Association of Business Communicators).

CASE 10 Westinghouse: Communicating for Productivity

A few years ago, at the Aerospace Electrical Division of Westinghouse (in Lima, Ohio), an intensive communication program was credited by company officials with being the prime cause of a 20 percent production increase in the space of eighteen months. According to Sharon Wheeler, manager of communication and community relations, productivity was measured straightforwardly, by dividing products manufactured by hours worked. The communication program (developed by an outside consulting firm), featured as its centerpiece the requirement that from one to three times each day each of the eighty supervisors had to conduct face-to-face discussions of "problems, procedures and progress" with each of his or her subordinates.

Another important part of the program, without which the required daily discussion might not have succeeded, was a series of training sessions (again, conducted by the consultants), attended by all supervisors and employees. These sessions came first in the program and were designed to improve interpersonal communication skills.
Source: IABC News, September 1980, pp. 1, 7 (published by the International Association of Business Communicators).

Understandably, we have no information regarding the *content* of the discussions between Westinghouse supervisors and employees beyond the vague reference to "problems, procedures and progress." The implication is that these discussions were conducted in a spirit of honest, two-way exchanges of views—that is to say, in a truly participative manner. We have no reason to believe otherwise. However, some companies have used similar "discussions" as a manipulative ploy, supporting an authoritarian or paternalistic management style.

Case 11 describes two slightly different versions of a device intended primarily to facilitate candid feedback from employees to management. Since the devices are so similar, experiences at two companies are combined in a single case.

CASE 11   TRW and General Electric: Getting Feedback from Employees Through Sensing Sessions and Roundtables

Both TRW and GE have earned national reputations for devising communication methods designed to obtain honest feedback from employees. TRW has used the labels *sensing sessions* and *one-in-five*. (The latter denotes the company objective of involving 20 percent of all employees as active participants in the sessions.) At GE the terms *roundtable* and *split-level* (referring to different hierarchical levels) have been used. TRW inaugurated its program around 1976; GE, many years earlier—in the 1940s (see Jones & Doyle, 1982, p. 58).

Typically, for example, at TRW, each sensing session is made up of a small group of employees and "conducted by a facilitator, who in turn makes a report to management." In this arrangement, employees do *not* deal directly with their immediate supervisors, so that the employees will feel free of inhibitions in voicing their comments or asking questions. At GE (1) employees are randomly selected, and their names are published in the company newspaper before the meeting takes place; (2) employees not selected are invited to submit questions to the participating employees; then (3) the plant paper (a weekly) publishes follow-up stories about what was discussed in the meeting, featuring many of the questions and answers.

In a 1979 news story, the reporter conceded that many employees persist in regarding sensing sessions as nothing but gripe sessions, even though TRW wants the meetings to provide a forum for employees to express opinions and ask questions going beyond the expression of immediate complaints. Robert Esposito, manager of training and organizational development at TRW's Reda Pump Division (Bartlesville, Oklahoma), has also admitted that some employees "view the sessions as an attempt by management to buy time on sensitive issues." Moreover, he says, while many employees find the sensing sessions "a positive experience," they have expressed the desire to deal with their immediate supervisors rather than with the facilitators.

Neither company, we should note, considers these meetings as any kind of cure-all for the myriad problems of internal communication. But they do view them as effective techniques for encouraging valid feedback from employees and obtaining employee evaluations of managerial performance.

Sources: Personal observation and discussions with corporate representatives; "Feedback Flourishes in Sensing Sessions," *IABC News*, May 1979, pp. 1–2.

You have read eleven episodes involving various facets of managerial communication. Just eleven. Clearly, these cases represent no more than an infinitesimal fraction of the total universe of managerial communication. They are both too few in number and too sketchy in detail to "prove" any laws accounting for either success or failure as an outcome of the ways managers communicate on the job. But at least they break the ice. They can start us thinking about the pervasiveness of communication phenomena in the life of any corporate manager.

We must acknowledge that these cases—like most published cases—suffer from two serious limitations. First, they focus primarily upon the more obvious and visible forms of communication. They typically do little to illuminate the less obvious, the less visible, the less structured types of communication events. (More about this in Chapter 3, which talks about the "visibility fallacy.")

Second, cases like these seldom report concealed, "backstage" communication behaviors, such as those involved in politicking, power plays, or manipulative games. Obviously, corporate politicians, power brokers, and Machiavellians do not shout their tactics from the rooftops. Yet I know that no reader of this book can fail to recall real-life examples of underground communication in corporate settings. In a later chapter we shall devote attention to internal politics, with special reference to implications for managerial communication. Meanwhile, if you have not already done so, you might want to look at two books that became quite popular during the 1970s: Jay (1974) and Maccoby (1976).

We have not yet arrived at a detailed, technical, dictionary-type definition of *communication*—managerial or any other kind. The most useful definition, in fact, will no doubt turn out to be an extended description of the phenomena we decide should be enclosed within the boundaries of the concept. For the moment, let it be enough to remind ourselves that the definitions people carry around in their heads can exercise a decisive impact upon their everyday behavior. Thus, if John Doe carries around in his head, as a part of his definition of communication, the notion that communicating means primarily "getting my message across to the other person," then this notion may be responsible for John Doe's overbearing monologues.

A dominant theme of this entire book will be that our assumptions and attitudes (frequently unstated or even unknown to ourselves) are commonly the culprits behind many deficiencies in the ways we communicate. Therefore, we shall be spending much of our time and energy on identifying and evaluating the assumptions (including informal definitions) lying beneath managerial communication behavior. We get started on this task in the next chapter.

Recommended answers to items in the Basic Communication Quiz: For all seven items, the best answer is **D—disagree.** For explanations, see later chapters.

References

Sources for the cases have been cited at the end of each case; hence, they will not be repeated here.

"Conversation with Reginald H. Jones and Frank Doyle." *Organizational Dynamics* 10, no. 3 (Winter 1982): 42-63.

Jay, Antony. *Management and Machiavelli: An Inquiry into the Politics of Corporate Life.* New York: Bantam Books, 1974.

Lewin, David. "Collective Bargaining and the Quality of Work Life." *Organizational Dynamics* 10, no. 2 (Autumn 1982): 37-53.

Maccoby, Michael. *The Gamesman.* New York: Simon & Schuster, 1976.

Nadler, David A., and Edward E. Lawler, III. "Quality of Work Life: Perspectives and Directions." *Organizational Dynamics* 11, no. 3 (Winter 1983): 20-30.

Parker, Mike, and Dwight Hansen. "The Circle Game." *The Progressive,* January 1983, pp. 32-35.

Watzlawick, Paul, Janet H. Beavin, and Don D. Jackson. *Pragmatics of Human Communication.* New York: Norton, 1967.

CHAPTER 2

On the Road to Self-Improvement: The First Step

THE NINE-STEP SCHEDULE: A PREVIEW

For managers who are serious about improving their communication effectiveness, this book advocates a specific, step-by-step program. The program is consistent with the four-stage cycle of human learning described by two well-known management authorities, Argyris and Schon (1974). Paraphrasing Argyris (1976, p. 37), we can visualize the most efficient learning as a cycle in which the learner progresses through these stages:

1. First, the learner identifies a problem.
2. Then the learner devises a solution.
3. Next, the learner applies the solution in actual behavior.
4. Finally, the learner "generalizes what has been learned to other settings."

While conceding that individual managers can, of course, make their own modifications in the nine-step schedule outlined below, I am convinced that something closely resembling this schedule will produce the best results. You will observe that some of the steps can be carried out only with the participation of other persons—as instructors, observers, critics, audiences, communicants.

In fact, as two experts on managerial training insist, no learning program should be attempted in a vacuum, but must "be viewed in the context of the organization as a whole." This means, in their words, that: "A manager or supervisor may need to learn how to communicate more effectively, but this training should not take place without the participation . . . of the rest of management, or the group of subordinates with whom he or she has to communicate" (Georgiades and Orlans, 1981, p. 137).

This chapter will deal with Step 1 of the nine-step schedule below. The remaining chapters will be relevant to those other steps which can be helped by reading a book.

Step 1: Raising Consciousness

In this earliest stage, you attempt to identify—in a preliminary and tentative way—communication problems, assets, and opportunities. Think of both your own personal behavior and the over-all corporate communication picture. (Consider the cases in Chapter 1 as examples of the kinds of events you might be looking for.)

Step 2: Identifying Assumptions

At Step 2 your purpose is to disclose basic beliefs likely to be influencing your ideas of what good communication is. These assumptions have an important impact, both on your personal communication skills and on the kinds of communication policies you establish in your areas of managerial responsibility. (This will be the subject of the next chapter.)

Step 3: Mapping the Territory

At the third stage you survey the skills, activities, and programs that represent the total territory of managerial communication. For convenience, this book will divide that territory into two major domains, to be labeled the *personal* and the *corporate*.

Step 4: Taking Aim

Steps 4, 5, and 6 spell out the phases of establishing your own personalized program for self-improvement. Preferably, you will consult other persons before setting up the final program. In Step 4 you learn the criteria by which to decide how closely managerial communication performance approaches the "ideal."

Step 5: Taking Inventory

Next you undertake a point-by-point comparison between what you are now doing and what—on the basis of the criteria identified in Step 4—you should be doing. You consider not only problems and difficulties, but you also take stock of what you honestly regard as your strengths. Moreover, you should not simply look at ways of doing better what you are already doing. Dare to consider whether some of these things should be done at all (for example, instead of merely improving your conduct of staff meetings, ask yourself whether the whole system of staff meetings should be abandoned in favor of a totally new approach). Clearly, Steps 4 and 5, although separated to ensure that careful attention is devoted to each process, are closely linked; you will find yourself slipping back and forth between them.

Step 6: Creating an Action Program

At this point you are ready to crystallize a specific, detailed set of learning activities. You must convert the results of your analysis in Steps 4 and 5 into a statement of all the concrete actions you propose to take. For instance, you might decide to enroll in a sensitivity training ("T-group") program, with the specific objective of improving your ability to listen empathically. Or you might decide to "study up" on the newest developments in office automation and their impact upon employee morale. In Step 6, then, you do not stop with formulating vague ideas in your head. You *commit to paper* a carefully written program of the learning experiences you intend to undertake.

Step 7: Practicing—in a "Safe" Environment

Step 7 involves actually putting into practice, either in a structured or an informal setting, the behaviors—and the attitudes—that represent your learning objectives. The important requirement here is that the environment be "safe." That is, you should try out your new skills under conditions where mistakes—which are an inherent part of the learning process—will not jeopardize your job or your interpersonal relationships. Such an environment might be a class, a workshop, or some sort of training laboratory. Sometimes it is also feasible to practice certain behaviors with the cooperation of colleagues, friends, or family members. An essential feature of all such practice is the provision of prompt and valid *feedback*. When a speaker gets information (whether accurate or not) regarding the way in which his or her message was received (if received at all), we call this feedback. Without feedback no learning is possible. (Hence instructors or consultants are frequently utilized in Step 7.)

Step 8: Applying What's Been Learned on the Job

Sometimes Step 8 is extremely difficult. Friends and co-workers, bosses and subordinates, and other associates may be puzzled by what they perceive as unexpected behavior. You may find it necessary to explain what's happening, to ask for patience, or even to engage in friendly debates. Indeed, you may have to attempt a campaign of reeducating some people—frequently a hopeless (not to mention antagonizing) endeavor.

(This problem demonstrates the wisdom of the experts who demand that managers, when undertaking a program of self-improvement, involve as many as possible of their on-the-job associates.)

Step 9: Seeking Continual Feedback

You might have thought that the schedule should end with Step 8. But to stop there would be to stop growing. Rather than resting on your laurels, keep checking up on yourself, looking for ways to enhance your communication skills even further. You should seek no stopping place, any more than good managers are willing to settle for a stopping place in company performance. So you find ways, both formal and informal, to obtain honest feedback regarding your communication effectiveness. These will range between formal attitude surveys and informal conversations with trusted associates.

Although a specified activity may be initiated at a given point in the schedule, you do not drop that activity before moving on to the next steps. You continue to give it attention from time to time throughout the entire sequence. At the late stages you are still reconsidering what you started in earlier steps. It's a cumulative process.

It's easy to assume that a self-improvement program like this one deals only with observable skills: writing letters, speaking before groups, conducting appraisal interviews, handling staff meetings, composing annual reports, producing closed-channel television shows, and so on. But such an assumption is false. It ignores the fact that learning new attitudes toward a manager's communication responsibilities is a crucial part—perhaps the most basic part—of an improvement program.

After conceding that the correlation between attitudes and behavior is far from perfect, we must acknowledge the indisputable facts that attitudes are among the most powerful determinants of behavior and that behavioral skills, when pursued as ends in themselves divorced from attitudes, become mindless charades.

IMPLEMENTING THE SCHEDULE

Recall Case 8 (Company F: The President and Personnel Manager), in Chapter 1. Aided by outside consultants, these two officers made earnest efforts to effect significant changes in two areas: (1) the over-all communication climate of the company (linked to a new management philosophy), and (2) the interpersonal relationship between them. They went through a prolonged learning period, following a regimen substantially the same as the nine-step schedule.

Outcomes were mixed. In the first area, a major shift did in fact seem to occur in the direction of open communication and a participative management style. In the second area, although there was progress in reducing misunderstandings and resentments, the two individuals were unable to resolve all their difficulties, and the personnel manager resigned—reminder, if we needed a reminder, that while striving for perfect solutions, we frequently must settle for something less than the happy ending to every scenario.

Consider now another case to add to those in Chapter 1.

CASE 12 Company H: The Vice-President's Memoranda

The officers in one division of Company H, a large corporation, consisted of a vice-president and fifteen directors reporting to him. As a part of a prolonged, corporate-wide organizational improvement program, these sixteen officers had participated in conferences and T-group (sensitivity training) experiences. Communication, both at the interpersonal and the company level, had been identified as a critical problem area. More specifically, interviews conducted by outside consultants had revealed that the fifteen directors all complained of difficulties in communicating with the vice-president. Some of the problems were said to be: (a) the vice-president was inaccessible; (b) the vice-president showed no interest in finding out what was on the directors' minds; and (c) the vice-president churned out an enormous number of memoranda, which were verbose, confusing, irritating, and insensitive (some directors protested that they spent "half the time" studying and responding to the memos).

We shall direct our attention to just one phase of the communication-improvement program: the vice-president's memos. The remedial techniques utilized in this phase, we should note, would almost surely have been impossible, were it not that all the individuals involved had already gone through rigorous, time-consuming T-group sessions. For it was in these sessions that all parties developed the ability to give and receive candid feedback regarding their communication behavior.

After the vice-president, in the presence of his fifteen subordinates, had agreed that the memos were an important component of a much deeper communication problem, the group generated a specific corrective program. Under the guidance of the consultants, the plan was put into practice. Among its most important features were the following:

Each subordinate was to provide the consultants with a copy of "the most confusing, irrelevant, or nonessential memo" the vice-president had sent him.

The vice-president was to do the same sort of thing—submitting "the most confusing, inadequate, or unsatisfactory reply he had received from each subordinate."

Then, in group sessions, the consultants would project each memo onto a large screen, so that everyone could study it. After reading the memo, each person would write what *he* thought the memo meant.

Each director was then to read aloud, to the entire group, what he had written. The original recipient of the memo was then called upon to describe his initial interpretation of, and response to, the memo at the time he received it.

Next, the vice-president himself was to be given the floor, to explain his intentions in writing the memo.

Finally, a free-wheeling discussion was to follow, in which everyone could suggest reasons for the difficulties and proposed solutions. (In these discussions, communication problems broader and deeper than just the memos were also considered.)

Because of time pressures, the group was unable to devote attention to memos and responses for every director. But the participant-observers (behavioral scientists) who authored the published report testified that, despite understandably high levels of anxiety on the part of all parties, unquestioned improvements occurred. As a single example, there was a dramatic reduction in the number of memos sent by the vice-president: in the six-month period preceding the experiment, the number was 367; six months later, it had dropped to 221; a year later, to 177.

Many basic communication problems were discovered and dealt with during the problem-solving sessions. It was found, for example, that the directors shared a common fear: If they asked the vice-president for clarification, they would be regarded as stupid. (The fear of asking what their bosses may perceive as "dumb questions" is widespread among subordinates in all kinds of organizations.)

Source: Jerry B. Harvey and C. Russell Boettger, "Improving Communication within a Managerial Workgroup," *Journal of Applied Behavioral Science* 7, no. 2 (1971): 164-79.

Many other procedures besides those described in Case 12 took place in the organizational improvement program. But this segment should be enough to suggest how ingenuity—combined with personal courage!—can be applied to implementing the nine-step schedule. In this particular instance, note especially the ways in which Steps 5 through 9 were exemplified.

We now turn our attention back to Step 1.

THE SCHEDULE: STEP 1—RAISING CONSCIOUSNESS

Reflecting upon the eleven cases presented in Chapter 1 provides practice in the kind of thinking that should characterize Step 1. By studying the cases, your mind should become attuned to identifying—in a preliminary and provisional way—analogous problems you could be facing in your own managerial life.

After all, you have to start somewhere. And the central idea of Step 1 is to sharpen your awareness of communication phenomena surrounding you. So you will ask yourself such questions as these:

- Is it possible that certain persons are persistently misinterpreting what I'm saying?
- Is it possible that I am misinterpreting what certain people are saying to me?
- What kind of communication climate do we have around here? (For example: To what extent do people feel free to ask questions, make suggestions, raise objections, express complaints, and so on? Do people feel emotionally secure, or is there an atmosphere of blaming, scapegoating, and self-defense? You might want to examine the Communication Climate Questionnaire in Chapter 8 for ideas on questions to ask here.)
- How effective am I in such situations as the following: conducting performance reviews with my subordinates; advocating a proposal with my boss; presiding over staff meetings; receiving complaints; writing memos; commending subordinates for good work; preparing reports; counseling employees or subordinate managers who are experiencing troubles on the job?
- Do I easily find out what's really going on around here? Or am I the last to know? How many informal contacts and friendships do I have at managerial levels like mine in other departments and at levels below mine, either in this department or elsewhere?
- Speaking generally, do people feel that they are receiving the information they need to perform their jobs?

- Are cliques or political alliances getting more than their fair share of the "goodies"? Are empire builders working at cross-purposes with the best interests of the company? Are prima donnas making life miserable for the rest of us? Is it conceivable that I myself am a prima donna?
- How do I fare when I have to negotiate with other managers to ask for help, or defend my own turf, or resolve disputes?
- And so on. Again, for more ideas, review the cases in Chapter 1 (as well as Case 12, above).

Do not assume that the job of diagnosis is complete at Step 1. You will continue to identify not only problems but strengths and opportunities as you progress through the schedule. Not until Step 5 will you be in a position to construct a reasonably definitive inventory of specific objectives. What you are doing in Step 1, although essential, is tentative and exploratory.

The strategy here is based upon the conviction that *too many self-improvement programs misfire* (sometimes even work harm) *because the manager has seized prematurely upon plausible but half-baked objectives.* Only after careful thought will you be in a position to articulate the learning objectives that are right for you. So keep your options open for a while.

A final word. Sometimes managers believe—or fear—that to improve their communication effectiveness they must effect a revolutionary change in their "personal style." True, changes will take place if improvement is to occur. However, all of us have acquired a number of ways of behaving that reflect the deepest recesses of our beings; and it is usually impossible—or of doubtful merit—to root out those ways and substitute different ones. In the last analysis, we must retain the attributes (the word *traits* is controversial) that make us recognizable as unique human beings. Therefore, the changes we undertake should be carefully interwoven into the fabric of our personalities.

John becomes a more effective John, but he is still recognizable as John. Mary is a more effective Mary, but still recognizable as Mary. In an article on managerial communication published in the *Harvard Business Review*, an experienced corporate executive put the issue neatly, under the heading "Be Yourself":

> Be yourself—whatever that is. Once subordinates have "read" a boss's personal characteristics and methods of communicating, a change of style or signals is destructive to the organization's goals. . . . Whether the supervisor is a Caspar Milquetoast or King Kong, he is most effective when using his natural personality. (Harriman, 1974, p. 145)

The next chapter will focus upon Step 2 in the schedule: identifying assumptions.

References

Argyris, Chris. "Leadership, Learning, and Changing the Status Quo." *Organizational Dynamics* 4, no. 3 (Winter 1976): 29-43.

Argyris, Chris, and Donald Schon. *Theory in Practice.* San Francisco: Jossey-Bass, 1974.

Georgiades, Nicholas J., and Vanja Orlans. "The Supervision of Working Groups." In *Social Skills and Work,* Michael Argyle, ed., pp. 116-143. London and New York: Methuen, 1981.

Harriman, Bruce. "Up and Down the Communications Ladder." *Harvard Business Review* 52, no. 5 (September-October 1974): 143-51.

Harvey, Jerry B., and C. Russell Boettger. "Improving Communication within a Managerial Workgroup." *Journal of Applied Behavioral Science* 7, no. 2 (1971): 164-79.

CHAPTER 3

Assumptions and Fallacies

THE SCHEDULE: STEP 2 — IDENTIFYING ASSUMPTIONS

Many problems commonly encountered in corporate communication are undoubtedly the direct result of beliefs and attitudes, rather than shortcomings in managers' behavioral skills.

It has been said before, but let it be said one more time, because the point is so very basic: the justification for occupying your time in examining assumptions—assumptions about human communication in general and about managerial communication in particular—is that you are getting at the roots of your everyday communication habits. Some of our assumptions are at the conscious level, frequently announced in dogmatic assertions. For example: "Most staff meetings could be abolished, and we'd all be better off." "The way to correct an employee's sloppy work is to call him in and read the riot act." "All managers worth their salt let their people know who's the boss." "When you're conducting an appraisal conference, use the 'sandwich technique': first tell 'em the good news, then lay out where they've got to improve, then conclude with praise and a pat on the back."

Other assumptions lie below the level of consciousness, rarely spoken out loud. Many times we even deny that we believe them. Examples: "My subordinates are no damn good." "Bootlicking is the only way to get ahead." "Bosses are patsies for flattery." "Nice guys finish last."

"Tact is a sign of weakness; tell it like it is." Who can doubt that beliefs like these are bound to have some sort of effect upon the way we "come across" to other people?

A recent article in the *Harvard Business Review* (Barnes, 1981) presented examples from contemporary corporate life to support essentially the same thesis this chapter is all about. "Like all people," Barnes wrote, "managers behave according to their assumptions of how the world works—whether, for instance it is a kind or a cruel place" (p. 108). The phrase "how the world works" includes, of course, how communication works.

The author chose to single out just three of many assumptions held, in his opinion, by large numbers of modern U.S. managers. He made the subtle but crucial point that, taken in isolation, a given assumption might not work any harm. However, when several assumptions are combined into an interlocking set, a dangerous situation may result. A combination of three such "harmless" assumptions does indeed cause managers to behave in a manner that creates a corporate climate of mistrust, Barnes argued.

Barnes also contended that many "correct" assumptions become "incorrect" when we try to apply them as inflexible, universal truths. Therefore, he urged managers to consider adopting the principle of "paradoxical action," which tells us that many generalizations about human behavior are best considered as paradoxes; for example, instead of assuming that delegation of authority is "good" or "bad," we might recognize that it is both good and bad.

The three assumptions singled out by Barnes, briefly stated, are (1) that issues important to managers "fall into two opposing camps," with the result that managerial decisions frequently are made on either/or grounds; (2) that "hard drives out soft," with the result that many managers believe a gun-slinging, "macho" style is the only way to manage; and (3) that "nice guys finish last," another way of saying that it's a cold, cruel world and that therefore it's dangerous to trust other people (Barnes, 1981, pp. 108-10). Each of these assumptions is sometimes true; to adopt their opposites as universal guides would be risky indeed. For example, we know that to trust *everybody* all the time on all matters can lead to disaster. But we also know what happens when the prevailing premise is "Trust no one." Barnes recommended that managers adopt the middle-ground assumption of *"tentative* trust." (To grasp the full import of Barnes's thinking, you will have to read the whole article.)

Near the end of the Barnes essay is a quotation from a company president who had just lived through a year of crisis in management-employee relations. "We lost contact," the president confessed, "[with] our own employees.... *We stumbled over our own assumptions*" (p. 116; emphasis added).

The remainder of the chapter will examine a special category of assumptions frequently entertained by managers. These assumptions are listed under the heading "fallacies"—fallacies about managerial communication. Will this chapter suggest that all management assumptions about communication are fallacious? Absolutely not. Probably our valid assumptions outnumber the false ones. But the false are the ones that cause trouble.

We shall also pay another visit to the Basic Communication Quiz (see Chapter 1), since the quiz includes assertions derived from several of these fallacies. This chapter does not, of course, terminate our concern with identifying assumptions. Later chapters will introduce additional assumptions for our contemplation.

MANAGERIAL COMMUNICATION: FOUR FALLACIES

1. The Back-Burner Fallacy

The manager harboring the back-burner fallacy is the one who believes: "My communication behavior will take care of itself. So long as I do a good job of managing, I can pretty well forget about my communication—it's something I can put on the back burner." Believe it or not, a surprisingly large number of practicing managers apparently subscribe to this view. They pooh-pooh the notion that skill in communicating with people is just as essential as expertise in finance, marketing, engineering, or what have you. Frequently these managers argue that, although communication competence is indeed important, most managers will automatically learn it through the process of living. Hence, any thought of spending time and effort on improving communication effectiveness can obviously be relegated to the back burner.

The Delegation Corollary. This fallacy can easily induce acceptance of a corollary, the delegation corollary, which is the comforting myth that managers can delegate their communication responsibilities to other people—such as secretaries, staff assistants, public relations officers, company editors, or attorneys. Managers frequently fail to realize that, whether they know it or not, and whether they issue statements or remain silent, their very presence communicates. As long as there exists a person to interpret a manager's behavior, the act of interpretation—of assigning meanings to that manager's behavior—will go on. Communication is taking place, regardless of the manager's intentions.

In like manner, when a representative does the talking in the role of surrogate for the manager, readers and listeners make note of that fact and draw their own conclusions. Some of the conclusions may be quite unflattering to the shadowy manager. In other words, delegating a communication chore to someone else is itself a communicative act.

To be sure, managers must ordinarily rely upon specialists for certain tasks requiring professional expertise: people who are trained as speech writers, editors, television technicians, and so on. But no one can substitute for the manager as an authentic human being, thinking and speaking and listening for himself or herself. Two researchers reported recently on their studies of several thousand employees of General Motors and AT&T. Their data were obtained (over a period of several years in GM) primarily from in-depth interviews, rather than superficial paper-and-pencil questionnaires (Goodman and Ruch, 1981).

Their most important finding? That "employees often don't even know the names of their top managers, but their *perceptions* of them are extremely important in forming attitudes about work" (p. 14; emphasis added). These perceptions were found to have more influence upon employees' over-all job satisfaction than "such important factors as salary, fringe benefits, job training . . . and company policies and procedures" (p. 15). On the basis of these perceptions, employees drew inferences about the effectiveness of top management. The research data indicated that the inferences would be negative unless the image of top management was one of over-all competence, combined with concern for employees as human beings.

A task force in TRW, assigned to develop a working draft of a five-year plan for employee communication, began the first paragraph of their report with this unequivocal declaration: "Every part of the managerial process . . . is dependent upon effective communication. Communication in the organization is the primary means by which we select, control and coordinate the activities of our human and material resources" (TRW Task Force, 1982, p. 1).

2. The Quick-Fix Fallacy

In a sense this fallacy is the flip side of the first. But instead of downgrading the importance of communication, the quick fix would have the manager believe that there is a communication magic. All the manager has to do is to learn the secrets—the word *secrets* keeps popping up in the promotional literature. Armed with these tricks, the struggling manager will master communication magic at once.

The mails are flooded with fancy brochures advertising communication nostrums, easily available on enrollment in someone's sure-fire course or purchase of someone's book of sure-fire recipes. Managers are assured, in the exact words of one sales pitch, that they will "come out ahead in every face-to-face situation." Examples of similar claims are plentiful. A few years ago an ad appeared in mass-circulation magazines, promoting a book that would enable the managerial reader "to learn, in just one hour, the secret (note that word *secret*) of how to command and dominate everyone you meet—right in the palm of your hand you hold the power to get your way with others every time." More recently, another book promised to go even further. It offered "a thrilling new concept of *psychological judo,* that shows you how to win people over to your point of view, no matter how antagonistic they've been to it before."

I am not suggesting that these short courses or popular books are devoid of useful instruction. However, some common themes running through them all are causes for concern. One is that the average mature adult can quickly and easily apply a set of prescriptions, thereby accomplishing the feat of turning around a lifetime of acquired habits. Another is that there really exist, locked away somewhere in a secret cabinet, communication techniques that absolutely guarantee success. And perhaps most dangerous of all are the definitions of this success. Almost invariably, success is measured by the extent to which one person can dominate others. No room here for acceptance of the integrity of other people. No room for open-minded exchange of ideas, for debate or discussion. No room for caring. Would you really want to work for a boss trained to think this way?

This book takes the position that human communication, especially in the volatile world of the corporate manager, is too complicated a matter to permit accepting a list of simple cookbook recipes as reliable guides for action. If there is a single Rock-of-Gibraltar principle (principle, not technique) governing all effective human communication, it is this: The communicator must *adapt* to the *specific* audience and *specific* situation. Looking for rules prescribing in precise detail how one should communicate, without exception and across all situations, is a quest doomed to failure. Principles yes, precise procedures no.

Finally, the ways in which mature adults behave in communication situations are generally so imbedded in their personalities that effecting major changes in communication habits requires time, frequently a very long time. Usually, significant modifications in communication behavior occur in small increments over periods of time. Almost always the quick fix is a delusion.

3. The Visibility Fallacy

The visibility fallacy is the one that makes it so easy for us to focus our attention upon the more obvious, the more familiar, the more visible communication events, while we neglect the subtle, the less conventional, and the less noticeable. Ask many managers what comes to mind when they think of the word *communication.* They will respond in terms of *communications* (with an *s*): memos, bulletin boards, telephones, videotapes, newspapers, and the like. Then, after a moment's reflection, they may add public speeches, formal meetings, informal conversations, interviews, suggestion systems, and perhaps even quality circles. A bit later they may mention rumors, press conferences, "Speak Up" programs, disciplinary actions, exit interviews, collective bargaining, and teleconferencing. There's nothing wrong with these responses as examples of important communication events, except one thing. They seldom go far enough.

Typically, we fail to realize the communication impact of such phenomena as how much time the boss spends on Topic A versus Topic B; what priorities govern which topics get discussed first and for the longest time in meetings; what kinds of questions are raised by a certain manager; what the minutes of a meeting include and what they exclude; a colleague's facial expressions and fidgets when Topic C is mentioned; who talks (unofficially, privately) with whom, about what, where, and when; which topics are *never* mentioned by Manager X; and much more. Nor do we typically consider as important communication dimensions of corporate life the cliques and alliances, the power blocs and political maneuverings, the distortions and suppressions of strategic information. We could go on, but this should be enough to alert you to what is meant by the less visible kinds of communication that comprise a vital component of corporate functioning.

In a widely cited article published a few years ago, T. J. Peters (a social scientist employed in a major consulting firm) argued convincingly that the managers who become aware of these less obvious forms of communication, and who learn how to exercise control over them, are the managers who really live up to their full potential (Peters, 1978). The apt title of his article was "Symbols, Patterns, and Settings: An Optimistic Case for Getting Things Done." I recommend it as required reading for all managers. (Not that I necessarily agree with everything Peters says, but only because his approach and his concrete examples will start the mental juices flowing.)

Another vigorous plea for managers to sharpen their awareness of the less visible communication events going on around them comes from a recent best-seller, *Corporate Cultures,* by Deal and Kennedy (1982). The first author is a Harvard professor; the second, a management consultant. Too many managers, these writers contend, "send a flurry of memos, letters, reports, and policy statements, hold pre-meetings, meetings, and management sessions where they use flip charts ... to accomplish ... well, sometimes they don't accomplish much" (p. 86). It is their opinion, based upon their studies of many U.S. firms, that perhaps as much as 90 percent of the really important decision making in the company is accomplished in the less formal modes and less formal communication settings.

30 Assumptions and Fallacies

They urge managers to think long and hard about what they call the "culture" characterizing a company or a unit within the company. They have in mind such things as the basic values and assumptions that account for the ways in which a company (or subunit) is managed, the persons regarded as "heroes," the "rites and rituals," and the informal networks (who talks with whom, about what, and so on). They urge managers to find ways of gaining admission into these informal networks. Only through them can a manager tune in on the stories, the rumors, the myths, the "inside dope," and the gossip—the messages that reflect the gut-level life of the company. Furthermore, by using his or her membership in informal networks, the manager can send up trial balloons before promulgating risky proposals, can deal with sensitive personality problems, and can hammer out policy differences in settings where people can make concessions without losing face.

Of special interest to readers of this book is the identification of distinctive communication roles performed by different individuals. These roles include—using the authors' special terminology—"storytellers," "priests," "whisperers," and "spies" (Deal and Kennedy, 1982, pp. 87–98). Persons performing such roles are carriers of vital cultural information, without which a manager is grievously crippled.

This topic will arise in a later chapter, to which further discussion is postponed. By now it should be clear how damaging the visibility fallacy can be.

4. The Conveyor-Belt Fallacy

According to the conveyor-belt fallacy, when human beings communicate they are transferring meanings—as by a conveyor-belt—from the mind of a message-sender to the mind of a message-receiver. Although a few minutes of thought is usually sufficient to expose the absurdity of this notion, large majorities of managers (and others, including students and professors) who attend workshops and training seminars agree with the conveyor-belt fallacy. How do we know this? Because, when responding to the Basic Communication Quiz (presented near the beginning of Chapter 1), they mark "agree" as their answer to Item 1. If you will look again at this item, you will see that it is an unequivocal affirmation of the conveyor-belt premise:

A (D) ? 1. When Person A communicates successfully with Person B, what has happened is that A has *transferred meanings* from A's mind to B's mind.

Apparently it does not occur to many people that, were this premise correct, there could be no misunderstandings between human beings, or between groups, or between nations! There would be no misunderstand-

EXHIBIT 3.1 The Double Interact

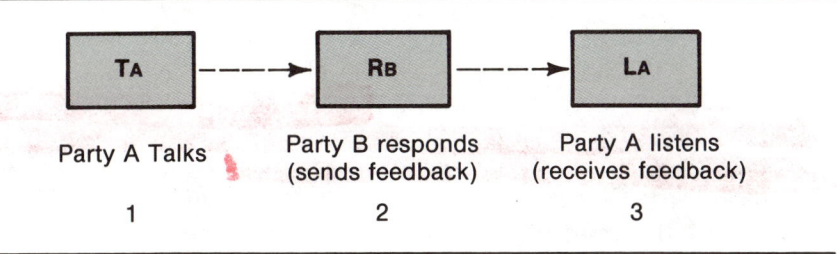

T_A → R_B → L_A

Party A Talks   Party B responds   Party A listens
                     (sends feedback)   (receives feedback)
      1   2   3

---

ing, for instance, between union and management representatives on the meaning of such terms as *solidarity, equal pay for equal work, incentives, productivity, profits, quota, loyalty,* and the like. And a phrase like *Zero Defects* would mean the same thing to rank-and-file workers as it does to managers (surveys have shown that in many plants *Zero Defects* means to the workers "Managers never make mistakes, only workers do").

Time now for a quick course in basic communication.

Let's start with what many social scientists call the basic building block, the minimal unit, of human communication: the *double interact.* This term describes a two-party situation. The parties may be individuals or groups or organizations—boss and subordinate, Production and Sales, management and labor. Party A sends a message (either verbal or nonverbal) to Party B; Party B responds in some manner (verbally or nonverbally); and Party A receives and interprets B's response. Using face-to-face conversation as a convenient example, we can visualize the three essential components of the complete unit as shown in Exhibit 3.1.

The communication circuit is broken if (1) Party B fails to receive the message, or if (2) Party B fails to emit any recognizable message in response, or if (3) Party A fails to receive B's feedback response, or if (4) Party A fails to comprehend that B's response really *is* a response to the original message that A sent.

Before going further, notice that in numerous companies incomplete or faulty double interacts characterize a great deal of corporate communication. Upper management, let us say, sends out a policy directive. Whether the statement is made orally or in writing, certain lower-level managers—and perhaps most employees—fail to receive it. Or if they do, they receive incomplete, garbled versions. In any event, the executives who issued the directive may receive either no feedback whatever or distorted feedback (especially if the feedback has been filtered through "yes-men").

Out of either indifference or fear, people may keep their mouths shut—except among themselves. At that level response may be voluminous and vociferous, but with none of it reaching the ears of top management. Human barricades may "protect" the executives from receiving unpalatable feedback originating at the lower levels of the company. (Recall Case 3 in Chapter 1: the president of Company B was sealed off from the middle manager's messages.) Sometimes the executives themselves may, because of either personality attributes or organizational tradition, discourage upward-directed messages. Even when the top officials are willing to listen to feedback, they may misinterpret it (this was part of the problem between the president and the personnel manager in Case 8).

Most damaging of all, in the absence of relevant feedback, management may exist in a fool's paradise, believing that its messages really have been received and understood. Then management plunges merrily ahead, making decisions and taking actions, all based on a delusion. Recall Case 4 from Chapter 1: the management of Company C, having announced a bad decision, belatedly solicited feedback, reversed gears, and closed the episode with the embarrassing—though courageous—confession, "We goofed!"

Make no mistake! *Without feedback, normal human interaction is impossible.* Even with feedback, a communicative act may go awry for a number of reasons. But the feedback is indispensable. (If the feedback is inaccurate or distorted, naturally there will be trouble. And there will be trouble if the sender of the original message misinterprets the feedback—which brings us to our next point.)

We have now completed the first half of the quick course in basic communication. The second half considers what happens when a message—whether original or feedback—passes from Sender A to Receiver B.

In a technical sense, all that is transferred between the two parties are physical manifestations of symbols. Words are probably the kinds of symbols that first come to mind. And the words, given recognizable form via sound waves (in speech) or light waves (in writing) are carried from A to B by any of numerous media: memos, bulletin boards, newspapers, in-house TV, loudspeaker, annual reports, employee handbooks, telephone, mass meetings, conversations, and so on.

Naturally, there are many symbols other than words: mathematical formulas, notation systems for the chemical elements, traffic lights, office furniture, modes of apparel, gestures, facial expressions, vocal intonations, handshakes, and so on. Do any of these symbols contain or transfer meaning from one person to another? No. They are stimuli; they *trigger* meaningful responses in the receiver, but they do not in themselves transfer meaning.

True, in everyday casual speech we commonly say that such-and-such a word (or some other symbol) "means" so-and-so. I don't propose to legislate against this convenient habit. But what we must do is realize that such usage encourages unconscious acceptance of the conveyor-belt fallacy. Think of a severely restricted symbol, where the meaning seems unequivocal, such as the symbol for sodium in chemistry: *Na*. This is a far cry from words like *democracy, love, conservative, liberal,* and even *management*. Could it not be argued that *Na* literally transfers the meaning *sodium* from Party A to Party B? Again, no. Does *Na* mean anything when presented to a ten-year-old who has never been exposed to chemistry? Well, it may mean something, but certainly not *sodium*. The only reason we can say that *Na* appears to mean *sodium* is that we (who have struggled through at least high-school chemistry) have been taught to respond with *sodium* when presented with the stimulus *Na*.

In like manner large numbers of people within any language community have been taught to respond in certain similar ways to the fairly large number of words that comprise what we call our *vocabulary*. But, even with the most familiar words, when we respond we are creating the meanings in our own heads. On what basis do we create the meanings? Only one basis is possible: the totality of our lifetime experiences, up to the present moment.

Insofar as two persons share similar lifetime experiences (and similar neurological equipment), they will produce similar responses to a given symbolic stimulus. Thus, English-speaking receivers will, upon seeing a certain animal, respond with the word *horse*. And when presented with the word *horse*, they will say that it means that animal. More properly, they have been taught—programmed if you will—to attach that meaning to the word. Spanish speakers, of course, will not create the same meaning for *horse* at all.

Even English-speaking people will not all have identical meanings for the word. Since no two human beings can be identical in terms of their lifetimes of experiences, they cannot have 100 percent identical responses (meanings). The ten years of my life spent in Los Angeles were unique to me; hence, in the most complete sense, *Los Angeles* will elicit a different meaning for me than for you. Even if you also spent ten years living in Los Angeles, our meanings will be different—although, to be sure, they will overlap.

It is the overlap in our life experiences, including things we have been taught, that makes possible understanding, and hence communication. Exhibit 3.2—admittedly oversimplified—may capture the main point. Circle A represents the meaning Party A associates with a symbol; Circle B, Party B's meaning. The shaded areas represent the overlap, or shared meaning, between A and B. (The common dictionary meaning— the formal definition—would be located as a tiny speck within the shaded areas, since it would represent only that part of the total possible meaning shared by all users of the dictionary.)

34 Assumptions and Fallacies

EXHIBIT 3.2 *Communication Overlap*

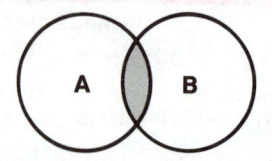

Narrow zone of overlap
(of shared experiences,
shared meanings)

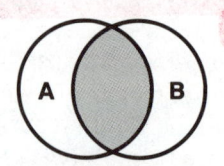

Broad zone of overlap
(of shared experiences,
shared meanings)

LOW LEVEL OF UNDERSTANDING   HIGH LEVEL OF UNDERSTANDING

The quick course in basic communication concludes with a dictum that Irving Lee, renowned teacher and semanticist, emphasized over and over throughout his distinguished career: *Words don't mean. People do.* Hence, avoid spending so much energy in asking what words mean, and ask instead what people mean.

Some Practical Consequences. If believing in the conveyor-belt fallacy made no difference in the way managers communicated on the job, we could forget about it. But compelling evidence, from both direct observation and research studies, suggests otherwise. Consider the following problems.

A. *The fallacy encourages managers in the dangerous belief that, just because they have spoken or issued a statement, they have successfully communicated.* I am reminded of a conversation with a corporate vice-president. He was telling me why he had "disallowed" a request for additional funds to hire more staff in the Employee Communications Department. "Why do we need all these postgraduate experts to tell me how to communicate? When I put out an announcement to the employees in this company—assuming they understand the English language and take the trouble to read it—I've communicated. There's no big mystery to justify keeping a bunch of overhead-staff people on the payroll." This is the conveyor-belt fallacy in its most pristine state. It assumes that the circles of meaning diagrammed in Exhibit 3.2 completely overlap.

The improbability of achieving such overlap is demonstrated by a famous field study conducted years ago (1961) by researchers from the University of Michigan. It's easy to assume that bosses who have previously occupied the same positions as those their subordinates now hold would surely be in an excellent position to understand the problems those subordinates face. Such, however, is not necessarily the case.

The researchers collected data, through in-depth interviews, from ninety-two superior-subordinate pairs in five companies. The investigators were surprised to find that whether the boss had previously held the subordinate's position or not made no significant difference in the degree of understanding between the two. And the degree of understanding was not generally high in any case. An earlier part of the same investigation had shown that more than two-thirds of the superior-subordinate pairs demonstrated "almost no agreement" with regard to the kinds of "obstacles" confronting the subordinate in performing his job (Maier et al., 1961).

A plausible explanation offers itself: despite obvious similarities, neither the experiences nor the perceptions of those experiences were the same for boss and subordinate. Moreover, if the organizational hierarchy works as it is supposed to work, the superior is not expected to understand the subordinate's problems in every detail. Were it otherwise, the boss would be inundated under an information overload, a point cogently argued by Rudolf Flesch (in Maier et al., 1961, pp. 60–67). We move on to another practical consequence of the conveyor-belt fallacy.

B. *The fallacy encourages a one-way approach to communication, thus discouraging a concern for listening or receiving feedback.* This, in turn, contributes to two closely related maladies of modern management: managerial insensitivity and managerial isolation.

Since the role of listening in managerial communication will be included in a later chapter, the topic will receive only brief treatment here. In general, listening can serve three functions for the manager: (a) to understand and retain information, (b) to analyze and criticize what is heard, and (c) to empathize with the other person. The best managers are good at all three kinds of listening. Frequently, however, managers who are skilled in one or two of these are not adept in the other(s).

Over the years surveys asking employees to describe their most effective bosses have commonly found that among the attributes at the very top of the list, "good listener" is consistently mentioned: "He's the kind of guy who will listen to you"; "She's the kind of supervisor who understands me when I try to talk to her"; "He's easy to talk to."

An integral part of good listening, of course, is the ability to solicit and accept feedback. There is nothing esoteric about the concept of feedback. What causes many communication fiascos is the practical difficulty encountered when we actually try to secure it. No wonder newspaper publishers, television advertisers, politicians—and corporate managements—spend millions of dollars every year in elaborate efforts to secure reliable feedback. How many managers find it easy to induce their subordinates to "tell it like it is," when the "it" refers to their evaluations of the manager's job performance? (For that matter, do most managers find it easy to give candid performance appraisals to their subordinates?) Recall such devices as the roundtables at GE and the sensing sessions at TRW (see Case 11 in Chapter 1). These are only two of numerous techniques designed to overcome the typical organizational barriers to upward-directed feedback.

A Cautionary Note. Beware of assuming that the only important feedback goes from employees to management. Feedback in the opposite direction is just as essential for organizational effectiveness. Performance reviews and MBO conferences are two familiar settings in which two-way feedback takes place (or, at least, should take place). We know that one of the surest ways of enraging (hence "demotivating") employees is the silent treatment from managers after those employees have tried to transmit urgent requests, reports, complaints, questions, or suggestions. Even a harsh answer is a response. No answer is worse, because it implies that the message sender is a nonentity.

Later sections of the book will have much more to say about all these matters, especially in relation to managerial insensitivity. For now, remember, while it is true that differences in meanings cause serious communication problems, if the parties are aware that such differences exist, they are at least in a position to do something about them. It's the unrecognized gap in understanding that causes the most grievous damage. William H. Whyte, Jr., formerly an editor at *Fortune* magazine, put it succinctly. *"The great enemy of communication,"* he said years ago, *"is the illusion of it"* (Whyte, 1952, p. 38; emphasis added).

The conveyor-belt fallacy may be the single most destructive, as well as the most widely held, of all assumptions causing managers to experience communication problems. Hence, the amount of space devoted to it here.

Look back now once again at your responses to the Basic Communication Quiz (Chapter 1). Earlier in this chapter we identified Item 1 as an encapsulation of the conveyor-belt fallacy, and therefore as a statement earning strong disagreement. You should now recognize Items 2 and 3 as corollaries flowing from this same fallacy:

A (D) ? 2. Effective communication can be boiled down to two essentials: first, Person A sends a message to Person B; second, Person B receives, understands, and acts upon that message.

A (D) ? 3. The ideal all-round communicator is one who (a) is intelligent and well informed; (b) uses language clearly and skillfully; (c) gains and holds the receiver's favorable attention;

(d) delivers his or her message in an interesting manner; and
(e) achieves the receiver's understanding and acceptance.

Both items provide admirable statements of important requirements for effective communication. But both items suffer from a fatal defect: they both fail to go far enough. Item 2 makes no mention of feedback, and Item 3 makes no mention of listening. Hence, despite their seductive wording, we are compelled to disagree with both items.

References

Barnes, Louis B. "Managing the Paradox of Organizational Trust." *Harvard Business Review* 59, no. 2 (March–April 1981): 107-16.

Deal, Terrence E., and Allan A. Kennedy. *Corporate Cultures—the Rites and Rituals of Corporate Life.* Reading, MA: Addison-Wesley, 1982.

Goodman, Ronald, and Richard S. Ruch. "In the Image of the CEO." *Public Relations Journal* 37, no. 2 (February 1981): 14-19.

Maier, N. R. F., R. L. Hoffman, J. L. Hooven, and W. H. Read. "Superior-Subordinate Communication." In *AMA Research Report no. 52* (New York: American Management Association, 1961), pp. 9-30.

Peters, Thomas J. "Symbols, Patterns, and Settings: An Optimistic Case for Getting Things Done." *Organizational Dynamics* 7, no. 2 (Autumn 1978): 2-23.

TRW Task Force on Employee Communication. Working draft of a proposed Five-Year Plan for Employee Communication in TRW. Cleveland: TRW, March 2, 1982.

Whyte, William H., Jr. *Is Anybody Listening?* New York: Simon & Schuster, 1952.

CHAPTER 4

The Manager's Communication Responsibilities

The first executive function is to develop and maintain a system of communication.

Chester I. Barnard (1938/1968, p. 226)

If communication is used to make the communicator look good, or feel big, or demonstrate superiority, it destroys its purpose.

Philip Lesly (1979, p. 199)

Before one sets out to improve his or her communication skills (or any other kind of skills) the wise thing to do, early in the game, is to conduct a reconnaissance of the kinds of activities the skills involve—in other words, to map the territory one will be traversing. This corresponds to Step 3 in the nine-step schedule (see Chapter 2), and it describes the central theme of this chapter.

Shortly, we shall see that the territory of managerial communication comprises two large domains. They will be labeled the *personal* and the *corporate*.

First, we examine what it means to be a manager.

WHAT DO MANAGERS DO WHEN THEY MANAGE?

Traditionally, writers on management theory have analyzed managerial work in terms of broad, abstract functions. Especially famous are the seven articulated by Luther Gulick in the 1930s, epitomized in the old acronym POSDCORB (Gulick, 1937, p. 13): **P**lanning, **O**rganizing, **S**taffing, **D**irecting, **C**oordinating, **R**eporting, and **B**udgeting. There is also the folklore captured in "The Six M's of Management": Men, Methods, Machines, Markets, Materials, and Money (the omission of women will be noted by readers of the 1980s!). Some contemporary companies have issued statements defining management by simply omitting three of the POSDCORB functions and retaining the other four: planning, organizing, coordinating, and controlling (on the assumption that controlling is synonymous with directing).

Although these functional descriptions have their uses in identifying what managers are supposedly attempting to accomplish, they have come under fire in recent years, primarily on two grounds: (1) that they take for granted the universality of the traditional bureaucratic structure (closely designed after the military model), and (2) that they tell us little about what managers actually do, what activities they engage in. Leading the charge, publicized in his award-winning 1975 article in the *Harvard Business Review*, has been a management professor from McGill University, Henry Mintzberg. The title of the article says a lot: "The Manager's Job—Folklore and Fact" (Mintzberg, 1975). And the concluding sentence of the article declares: "It is time to strip away the folklore about managerial work, and time to study it realistically...."

Mintzberg's basic thesis is that we must scrutinize, in minute detail, the daily activities of flesh-and-blood managers; then, on the basis of such data, we can construct catalogues of specific skills a manager needs to master.

Mintzberg identified in his 1973 book five kinds of behavior—all of them involving some form of communication, whether sending or receiving. He observed five chief executives during their entire workdays, for five weeks, and tabulated their acts minute by minute, summarizing his data under five "media activities." In descending order according to percentage of the managers' total time spent on each, these activities were:[1]

Attending formal, scheduled meetings	59 percent (of total time)
Handling incoming mail and the like	22 percent
Attending informal, unscheduled meetings	10 percent
Talking on the telephone	6 percent
Making "tours" (visits to others)	3 percent

---
[1] Summarized from data reported in Mintzberg, 1973, pp. 38–44.

Mintzberg regarded as "the most significant finding" concerning these activities the fact that the managers spent approximately four-fifths of their workday (78 percent of their time) in *oral communication* (p. 38). Two other notable facts emerged:

- The managers placed high priority upon keeping abreast of the most recent ("hot") information—typically received through informal contacts in unscheduled meetings or by phone.
- A very important part of "the manager's information diet" consisted of messages characterized by considerable uncertainty—such as "gossip, speculation, and hearsay" (see Mintzberg, 1973, p. 36).

A conclusion of overpowering significance can be stated in this single sentence: "The manager's activities are characterized by *brevity, variety,* and *fragmentation*" (Mintzberg, 1973, p. 171; emphasis added). For example: "half of the observed activities were completed in less than nine minutes, and only one-tenth took more than an hour" (p. 33). We should note that, although Mintzberg's primary data were derived from only five CEOs, he was able to cite similar findings from several earlier investigators, who studied supervisors and middle-line managers as well as top executives. We can conclude that the typical manager's day is likely to be a kaleidoscope of disjointed communication events, rapidly tumbling one upon the other.

Of one fact we may be certain: the "manager's work is primarily oral" (Georgiades and Orlans, 1981, p. 117). In Mintzberg's words, "Unlike other workers, the manager does not leave the telephone or the meeting to get back to work. Rather, these contacts *are his work*" (1973, p. 44). After agreeing that most of the manager's day is indeed spent in oral communication, Davis and Luthans observe that all this communicating consists chiefly of "persuading, justifying, and legitimizing past, present, and future courses of action" (1980, p. 65). This remark moves us from the lower analytic level of description (looking at observable behavior) to the higher level of inference—asking what purposes or functions are served by the behavior. (In a sense, despite the criticisms of Mintzberg and others, we come back to something like POSDCORB!)

EXHIBIT 4.1   A Disturbing Thought

If Mintzberg and other researchers are correct, are we not justified in suspecting that most managers have neither the time nor the energy to focus thoughtful analysis upon the major problems confronting them? As Mintzberg suggests, the manager is preoccupied with the "current and tangible," whereas "the complex problems facing many organizations call for reflection and a far-sighted perspective" (1973, p. 173).

THE ROLES OR PURPOSES OF MANAGERIAL WORK

In the 1960s, theorists dissatisfied with the traditional POSDCORB taxonomy proposed other categories for analyzing what it is that managers "really" do. These theorists cast their categories in terms of roles. The role concept is closely related to purposes, objectives, and functions. For example, Sayles (1964), after observing the work of lower-level supervisors and middle-level managers, proposed that managerial activity could be characterized in terms of three types: (1) "participant in external work flows" (which includes such activities as "trading," advising, and innovating), (2) leader, and (3) monitor. A few years later Rosemary Stewart (1967) conducted an intensive investigation of 160 middle- and senior-level managers, emerging with five basic "job profiles" or roles: (1) emissary, (2) writer, (3) discusser, (4) trouble shooter, and (5) committeeman.

Now we come once more to Mintzberg. In his 1973 book he elaborated upon a set of ten managerial roles, classified under three categories of activity (see Mintzberg, 1973, especially pp. 54–99). These are listed below:

Activities involving interpersonal relationships:
1. Figurehead (performing ceremonial, symbolic duties).
2. Leader (staffing, training, directing subordinates).
3. Liaison (maintaining contacts with "outsiders").

Activities involving information transfer:
4. Monitor (receiving information).
5. Disseminator (sending information).
6. Spokesman (transmitting information to outsiders).

Activities involving decision making ("strategy-making"):
7. Entrepreneur (initiating change).
8. Disturbance handler (taking corrective action).
9. Resource allocator (acting as "heart" of corporate strategy).
10. Negotiator (negotiating with both "internal" and "external" parties).

That all these roles require the manager to be, above all else, a communicator is clear.

It is time now to examine in some detail exactly what it is that managers do when they communicate. We need to be more specific than saying merely that managers speak, write, read, and listen. Thus, we need to map the territory of managerial communication.

THE SCOPE OF MANAGERIAL COMMUNICATION

In the light of all that has been said in Chapter 3 and in the preceding pages of this chapter, we should first remind ourselves that, without stretching the term to the point of vacuity, we can properly regard any or all of the following phenomena as examples of communication:

1. Message-sending, both intentional and unintentional.
   A. Messages comprise:
      Human behavior, both verbal (spoken or written) and nonverbal (including voice, gesture, apparel and the like).
      Nonhuman objects or events (buildings, work areas, office furniture, use of color, and so on).
2. Message-receiving, whether desired by the sender or not.
   A. Ways to receive identifiable messages or message events include:
      Listening (in both formal and informal contexts—hence, includes listening to gossip and rumor).
      Reading (newspapers, memos, reports, notices on bulletin boards, posters, and so on).
      Observing (nonverbal human behavior, nonhuman objects or events).
      Engaging in combinations of the above (viewing closed-circuit TV productions, going on field trips or site visits, and so on).
   B. Generalized responses and over-all impressions (not associated with particular messages or message events) are also a part of message-receiving. Examples include:
      Perceptions of corporate management's image.[2]
      Impressions of the "corporate-communication climate" (as perceived by various groups of employees, managers, customers, suppliers, and the like).

It is also possible—and, in many situations, very important—to consider two other dimensions of messages:

- Are they *original* messages (as arbitrarily identified in any specified series of communicative acts)?
- Or are they *feedback* messages (relating to how the original messages were received)?

As if all this were not enough, we must remember that messages can be transmitted or exchanged in an almost endless number of ways (keeping in mind, from the discussion of the conveyor-belt fallacy in Chapter

---

[2] Recall the research findings by Goodman and Ruch (1981), reported in Chapter 3, regarding the impact of top management's image upon employee attitudes.

3, that only the physical representations of symbols, never the meanings themselves, are transmitted!). Managers, when giving thought to the totality of corporate communication, find specific examples of communication activities categorized under such headings as the following:

1. **Media**—the physical carriers of messages.
   A. *Mass media* include:
      Newspapers and other publications for employees or management, bulletin boards and posters, "pay inserts," loudspeaker systems, telephone "call-in" recordings, in-house closed-circuit television, speeches and announcements, published union contracts or agreements, public media used for corporate communication purposes, and so on.
   B. *Media directed to individuals* (either singly or in small groups) include:
      Face-to-face conversations; person-to-person telephone calls; memos and letters; confidential reports; meeting notices, agenda, and minutes; and so on.
2. **Channels**—the ways in which senders and receivers are linked, or the ways in which communication of information is routed from one person (or group) to another. The following are some of the useful distinctions to be made:
   A. *Official (formal)* "chain-of-command" channels run from the top to the bottom levels of a conventional hierarchy (in the traditional bureaucratic structure, the channels are predominantly vertical rather than horizontal or diagonal).
   B. *Unofficial (informal)* channels run in all possible directions—up, down, across, diagonally—and frequently include "outsiders."
   C. *Direct* channels contain no intervening links.
   D. *Indirect* channels include one or more intervening links, or "relays," between a message source and an intended message destination.
   E. *Functional* networks (either formal or informal) may have to do with production, research and development, marketing, forecasting, finance, purchasing, personnel selection, grievance procedures, suggestion systems, and so on. Also, they may involve such unofficial groupings as cliques, friendship circles, alliances, coalitions, "rumor mills," clandestine intelligence-gathering arrangements, gossip chains, and the like.
3. **Audiences**—the intended receivers of messages, including single individuals. Note the word *intended*. Every manager is familiar with the fact that many messages reach audiences other than those intended. Indeed, many times the unintended audiences may outnumber the intended.
   A. *Internal* audiences include:
      Rank-and-file employees—either as a total group or in specified

segments (along departmental, functional, professional, and other lines)—and first-level supervisors, middle-level managers, and top managers and executives, whether line or staff.
B. *External* audiences include:
Targeted community leaders; educators; students; potential customers or clients; government officials; specified pressure groups; specified minorities, by sex, by race, by physical handicap, and so on; and others, as circumstances dictate.

Further, all those listed as internal audiences can also be listed as external ones, since they all are members of the general public when they are not on the job. Hence, they receive information (whether accurate or not) regarding the company from commercial newspapers, professional journals, radio and TV, friends and neighbors, competitors, and so on. Many managements ignore this fact!

C. *Intermediate* audiences (outsiders closely linked to the company for a variety of special reasons) include:
Present and past customers and clients, union officers, suppliers.

EXHIBIT 4.2 A Comment—and a Warning

A recent survey of almost fourteen hundred professional communicators (members of IABC, the International Association of Business Communicators) revealed that numerous companies are issuing publications specifically tailored for special audiences—in addition to the usual general-employee audience (Zuegner, 1980).

It becomes immediately obvious that adapting to many unique audiences requires communication skills of the highest order. It's also obvious that the average manager will need to call upon specialists—not to assume managerial communication responsibilities (as in the delegation corollary of the back-burner fallacy, described in Chapter 3), but to render assistance. An especially acute problem arises in the need to avoid contradictions, or the appearance of contradictions, among messages addressed to different audiences.

Hence the warning: All too often corporate managements (and even their staff specialists, who should know better) behave as though they think employees never read metropolitan newspapers or listen to the TV evening news. Thus, we have the spectacle of Company X representatives' being quoted, in the downtown financial pages, on the healthy financial picture for the current year—at the same time the employee "house organ" pushes alarmist rhetoric about the need for belt-tightening, austerity, and cost-cutting.

The crux of the matter is to say *different* things (at times) to different audiences, while never saying *incompatible* things to them. Only top management is in a position to coordinate the main themes of all corporate communication, so that internal and external messages are never inconsistent.

consultants, current or potential job applicants, shareholders, retirees, dealers, and so on.
4. **Modalities**—sensory-receptor systems whereby the normal human being is made aware of environmental inputs. Although all the senses are involved, at one time or another, as receptors of incoming messages, the two most dominant are obviously *sight* and *hearing*. The research literature on the relative advantages and disadvantages of receiving written versus oral information is extensive, complex (and frequently contradictory). Here again managers can seek help from those with special expertise. A readable and nontechnical summary, although a few years old now, is provided by Travers (1970).
5. **Methods, techniques, formats**—the almost infinite number of ways in which it is possible to "package" a communication event. For an account of a whole program, conducted over a period of two years and involving an ingenious mix of various techniques, see Case 5 in Chapter 1, on the relocation of AT&T Long Lines. Listed here is a brief sampling of the multitude of possibilities.
   A. *Quality circles:* see Case 2 in Chapter 1.
   B. *Delphi groups:* problem-solving groups whose members are dispersed, never meeting face to face during the process. Ideas are solicited and sent to a central coordinator, who collates and summarizes them, then sends the summary back to the members. The members react to the summary, evaluate all the ideas, and send their reactions back to the coordinator. The coordinator once more collates and summarizes, returning the results of this process to the members—who react and evaluate again. The whole procedure continues in like manner for several "waves," until an acceptable stability of response is reached—or until everyone gives up in exhaustion!
   C. *Brainstorming:* a technique, originally developed in Madison Avenue ad agencies, designed to encourage free-wheeling generation of creative ideas, the wilder the better. A key feature is the absolute prohibition of any critical comments, objections, or arguments until the end of the idea-generating phase.
   D. *Roundtables and sensing sessions:* see Case 11 in Chapter 1.
   E. *Question-and-answer programs:* techniques coming in a bewildering variety of shapes, with about as many differences as there are companies using them. Some of the best known are "Speak Up!" at IBM, "Hotline" at General Electric, and "Inside Line" at Honeywell. Typically, elaborate measures are utilized to ensure anonymity to employees asking sensitive questions or raising harsh complaints; and prompt, substantive answers are provided by high-ranking managers (with answers likely to be of wide interest published in company newspapers).

EXHIBIT 4.3   Two Examples of Ingenious Use of Videotape

Ohio Bell, in February 1980, inaugurated a multifaceted communication program intended to provide company information to more than four thousand employees of one division. The program, called RSVP, has as its centerpiece a monthly videotape, usually about twenty minutes in length, containing such features as "news clips, an executive forum, in-depth analysis of single issues, feedback acknowledgments and responses," and problems in the sales or service areas. The videotapes are supplemented by discussion groups, feedback forms, and newsletters (Coyle, 1981).

At AT&T, marketing people were shown a videotape of a real-life customer making a complaint about telephone service. This technique succeeded in bringing "the customer's anxiety and rage to the people who have to fix it," according to Mike Forney, manager of employee communications *(Ragan Report,* Nov. 23, 1981, p. 2).

F. *"Confrontation meetings":* a device named and invented by Beckhard (1967), featuring such elements as insistence upon complete candor in identifying company problems and failures, strict enforcement of the rule against penalizing anyone for candor, and intensive small-group discussions. For a detailed description, see Beckhard's original article in the *Harvard Business Review,* 1967.

G. *Videotaped discussions, role playing and the like:* for example, some companies involve top executives in unrehearsed, videotaped panel discussions with employees. The tapes are then shown on TV monitors in various locations. Thus, remote executives, instead of being faceless names, are seen as flesh-and-blood human beings.

If a manager, reading all the categories and items listed above, should conclude that communication in the corporate setting encompasses an enormous area—far too extensive for any single manager to master thoroughly—he or she would be absolutely right. Not even a communication specialist sporting a Ph.D. degree could be expected to possess expertise in all the media, all the modalities, all the methods. What, then, is reasonable to expect of the typical manager? The following should be the minimum:

1. Every manager needs to be at least adequate in using the basic oral and written communication skills (grammar, language, voice, oral delivery, and so on).
2. Every manager needs to be an efficient reader and an empathic listener.
3. Every manager needs to understand the communication implications of corporate policies and decision making.

4. Every manager needs to be aware of the innumerable communication roles, or obligations, involved in his or her interpersonal relationships with superiors, peers, subordinates, and others.
5. Every manager needs to think through the kinds of communication policies and programs that the company—or a specified subdivision of the company—should be adopting.
6. Every manager needs at least a general understanding of the numerous ways in which communication can be enacted (the media, the modalities, the audiences, and the methods enumerated above). As a corollary, the manager must see the linkage between corporate needs and the ways in which communication can serve those needs. Without being an expert in any of the media specialties, the manager should be sufficiently knowledgeable to make sensible recommendations and to evaluate the over-all appropriateness of the techniques proposed by specialists.

Any manager who is not meeting these six minimal requirements will fall short of fulfilling his or her potential as a managerial communicator—hence, as a manager. To facilitate the mastery of these essential communication competencies, the manager will find it useful to analyze the totality of managerial communication not so much in terms of endless lists but as a territory divisible into two domains. As mentioned earlier, convenient labels for these are the *personal* and the *corporate*.

THE TWO DOMAINS OF MANAGERIAL COMMUNICATION

Familiar to all of us are such comments as the following: "As a person I like him, but as a boss he's a flop"; "She knows what's needed, but she can't make anyone understand what she's driving at"; "He does the best he can with these performance reviews, but corporate policy puts him in a bind." To shift perspective, imagine the situation in which two managers find it necessary to advocate a proposal for a new program. Boss A makes a cogent and highly persuasive presentation at a staff meeting. Boss B, with the same facts available, succeeds in antagonizing those listeners whom he has not put to sleep. Or, consider another manager who is known as an unusually charming, polished speaker. But she's the same manager who fails to grasp the necessity of keeping employees well informed of company plans and prospects. Hence, she may keep the plant editor on a shoestring budget, withhold approval of materials for the bulletin boards, or argue against investing funds in a closed-circuit television capability.

These are manifestations of the fact that a manager may be highly effective in one aspect of communication performance, but inadequate in another. In postulating two fundamentally different—albeit frequently overlapping—dimensions of managerial communication, I hasten to emphasize this point: No impenetrable barrier exists between the two. Think of this analogy. East is a direction diametrically opposite to west. Yet, no one can draw a line (except arbitrarily, on a map) and declare: This is where east begins and west ends. East and west are on a continuum, rather than being two separate, airtight compartments.

In like manner, we can visualize two different directions in which a manager's communication efforts can move: the personal and the corporate. Examine Exhibit 4.4. You will observe that it treats these two aspects of managerial communication as two domains of a larger territory, the territory of managerial communication.

Note that these domains are separated not by a vertical but by a diagonal line. Thus, in almost any single communication episode, the manager's total communication behavior can be analyzed in terms of varying proportions of the personal and the corporate components. The vertical dotted line (X) designates a communication episode—for example, a performance appraisal conference—in which the mix of communication skills is roughly two-thirds corporate and one-third personal. In real life we seldom encounter examples of managerial behavior in which either the personal or the corporate component is totally missing.

What is being proposed here is that the two domains represent combinations of attitudes, talents, and insights sufficiently different from each other to warrant devoting attention to them as separate entities—even though, in everyday situations, the two elements are always mixed in varying proportions. You will see that the personal domain reflects that part of a manager's behavior deriving primarily from his or her unique personality, without regard to the particular job or position the manager happens to occupy. The corporate domain reflects that part of the manager's behavior deriving primarily from the position (or role) he or she occupies.

One way of understanding the practical importance of differentiating the personal and the corporate dimensions is to consider the contrast between two hypothetical managers, Manager A and Manager B, in a specific communication situation. Let's take one of the most common (and one of the most difficult) communication tasks that managers face: conducting a performance appraisal (or "review") with a subordinate. Let us suppose that Manager A is highly skilled in carrying out the company's directives regarding performance reviews. She is widely praised for her ability to empathize and to create an atmosphere free of

EXHIBIT 4.4 The Two Domains of Managerial Communication

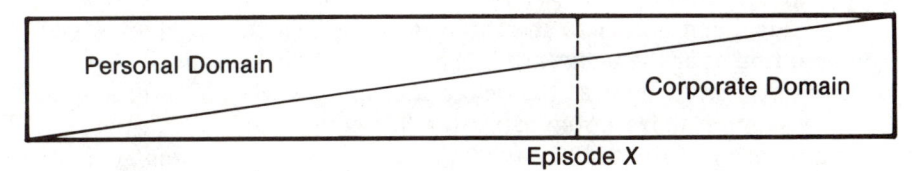

Personal Domain	Corporate Domain

Episode X

In this hypothetical on-the-job episode, Episode X, the mix of the manager's communication behavior is about two-thirds corporate and one-third personal.

Manager's Behavior Perceived in Terms of His or Her Unique Personality	Manager's Behavior Perceived in Terms of His or Her Position, Role

DIRECTLY OBSERVABLE SKILLS
  Speech communication—basics.
  Written communication—basics.
  Discourse technique (oral or written)—persuasion, exposition, negotiation, and the like.
PERSONAL ATTRIBUTES (INFERRED)
  Assumptions, attitudes, intelligence, self-esteem, ethics, and the like.
MANIFESTATIONS
  In office (or equivalent) settings—manager's office or other party's workplace.
  In one-on-one situations (dyads)—face to face meetings, phone calls, memos, letters, and the like.
  In small groups (usually three to about fifteen persons)—as leader or as member.
  Through primarily one-way message sending—small, informal meetings or audiences, large meetings or audiences, or media.
	DIRECTLY OBSERVABLE PRODUCTS
	  Documents (corporate prose)—manuals, policy statements, rules and regulations, mass media (print, electronic), and the like.
	  Channels, networks, media—links in chain of command, information dissemination networks, print and oral media, and so on.
	  Communication practices, devices, methods, techniques—performance appraisals, sensing sessions, quality circles, suggestion systems, "Speak-Up" plans, counseling programs, and the like.
	INTENTIONS, GOALS, ASSUMPTIONS, PHILOSOPHY (INFERRED)

threat, so that subordinates can express themselves honestly and come to grips with their problems.

Manager A is successful, then, in fulfilling the requirements of her corporate communication role. She is careful, for example, never to allow the appraisal conference to slip into something resembling a tête-à-tête conversation over the backyard fence. Nor does she conduct a performance review as if it were a cross-examination in a criminal prosecution. But she is even more noteworthy for her command of such personal communication skills as listening more than talking, avoiding dogmatic assertions, using open questions, and applying techniques like verbalizing the subordinate's unstated feelings or asking neutral, nonthreatening questions to facilitate relevant self-disclosure.

Manager B, on the other hand, leaves much to be desired in his person-to-person communication behavior. He tends to be unduly brusque; he has a loud, harsh voice; and, when he addresses an audience or a staff meeting, he rambles aimlessly from point to point, gets himself entangled in involute sentences, and interlards his discourse with hundreds of *uh*'s. However, Manager B was also the driving force behind installing the highly successful performance review program. He is the chief author of the company manual—he literally wrote the book on this subject. He is known for his far-ranging, inquisitive mind and for his understanding of all the latest thinking in management theory.

In short, Manager B is no better than mediocre in certain personal communication skills—those aspects of his behavior independent of his corporate position. But, in at least one critical area of corporate communication, he has made a signal contribution. He was able to apply the fruits of one personal communication skill—the ability to read and retain what he reads—to the generation and articulation of a highly regarded performance review policy. It also turns out that, despite his shortcomings as a speaker, Manager B is able to listen, with a mind open to new information and unorthodox ideas. This is another personal communication skill in which he excels, and it contributes mightily to his outstanding success in promulgating the performance review program, the crowning achievement of his corporate communication performance.

Although both the personal and the corporate skills are manifested in both person-to-person settings (such as conversations) and nonpersonal settings (such as policy manuals or employee newspapers), in general it can be said that the personal skills predominate in person-to-person situations and the corporate skills in nonpersonal ones. In the case of our hypothetical managers A and B, it is clear that A surpasses B in most (but not all) of the personal, whereas B may surpass A in some (but not all) of the corporate. A partial grading report on these two managers might look like Exhibit 4.5.

To ask which of these two managers is the better over-all managerial communicator is not to ask the most useful question. These personal

EXHIBIT 4.5 Partial Evaluation of Two Hypothetical Managers' Communication Skills

Scale: 10 = high; 1 = low	Manager A		Manager B	
PERSONAL COMMUNICATION				
Speech communication:				
Speaking	Very good	9	Mediocre	3
Listening (empathic)	Superb	10	Adequate	5
Listening (to dissent and new ideas, concepts)	Good	8	Superb	10
Written communication:				
Writing	Adequate	5	Good	8
Reading	Adequate	5	Superb	10
Discourse techniques:				
Explaining ideas clearly	Superb	10	Fair	4
Persuading	Good	8	Good	8
Counseling (as in performance appraisal)	Superb	10	Fair	4
CORPORATE COMMUNICATION				
Understanding and devising communication policies, plans, methods	Adequate	5	Superb	10

and corporate abilities are not the kinds of things that can be added up like the items listed in a printout from the supermarket cash register. More to the point is using the personal/corporate model as a convenient device for breaking down the amorphous concept *managerial communication* into two dimensions that represent significantly different competencies.

Now is an appropriate time to go back once more to the Basic Communication Quiz in Chapter 1. Look at Item 4:

A ⓓ ? 4. Communication skills, once mastered, are such that the person who is an effective communicator in one type of managerial situation will *almost* always be an effective communicator in other managerial situations.

No further discussion should be needed to justify a *D-disagree* response. In fact, it is an extremely rare individual who is equally proficient in both the personal and the corporate domains, or even in all the different skills included in one of the domains. Good talkers are frequently not good listeners (regrettably). And good interviewers are not necessarily good generators of companywide communication policies—such as feedback systems, performance review systems, guidelines for the company magazine, and so on.

The most effective managers are those who can sense the communication demands of a given situation and then call upon the appropriate mix of personal and corporate skills for that situation. I know of a case in which a multi-million-dollar gift to a university resulted from a person-to-person chat on the golf course. This occurred, however, after two or three years of inconclusive and frustrating "official" (corporate) communication encounters between the donor and the university vice-president.

At this point it is instructive to reread the twelve cases presented in the preceding chapters, analyzing them now in terms of the differences between the personal and the corporate domains. For example, look at some cases from Chapter 1:

Case 1 (Company A: Manning the Barricades). As individuals, most of the managers I met in Company A were skillful personal communicators. But they were struggling to survive in a flood of bad corporate communication. A training course in interpersonal communication skills would have been irrelevant. What was called for was a major focus upon changing the premises underlying the whole corporate communication climate. (Whether, short of wholesale firings of managers, this change could have been accomplished is a moot question.)

Case 3 (Company B: The Management Maze). We may suspect that the middle managers who built the protective wall around the company president were victims of myopic corporate (not necessarily personal) communication policies.

Case 5 (AT&T Long Lines: Moving and Communicating). The great variety of methods used by AT&T Long Lines, all coordinated in a carefully designed two-year program, demonstrates command of numerous corporate communication skills. Of course, personal skills were also involved in writing the various printed materials and in conducting the face-to-face meetings.

Case 8 (Company F: The President and the Personnel Manager). Although both personal and corporate deficiencies contributed to the messy situation in Company F, the most critical failures were, in my judgment, in the personal area. Within that area, the problems of neither the President nor the PM lay in basic speech skills. Both individuals were highly articulate; both could express themselves clearly and forcefully. However, the mental states—those perceptions, assumptions, and evaluations lying behind their utterances—produced an escalating spiral of mistaken perceptions, which in turn distorted their listening (they heard the "wrong things"), which in turn caused them to experience difficulty in saying what really needed to be said. Despite a history of personal friendship between them, these two people required the intervention of an outsider before they could begin to "level" with each other—and even then they never completely succeeded in achieving reciprocal understanding.

We could go on with the remaining cases, but space limitations prohibit it. Note well that the corporate domain is particularly involved in the *conceptual* or *philosophical* aspects of communication. This is not to derogate the "action" skills required to publish a plant newspaper, produce a videotape, and so on. Such skills are essential, but they must be preceded by work at the conceptual level. Action there must be, but policy should come first.

Having mapped the territory of managerial communication, the chapter concludes with a checklist tying everything together in terms of the manager's communication responsibilities. These responsibilities lie primarily in the corporate domain.

THE MANAGER'S CORPORATE COMMUNICATION RESPONSIBILITIES

A Strategic Question

Whenever anyone talks about managerial responsibilities or managerial work, the implicit assumption seems to be that all managers, because they are managers, perform essentially the same duties. In fact, this is exactly the assumption underlying both the traditional POSDCORB functions and the managerial roles of Mintzberg.

A highly respected team of researchers, Katz and Kahn (at the University of Michigan), have questioned this premise. They have proposed a theory of managerial leadership based upon the postulate that leadership styles and methods vary systematically according to the hierarchical level of the manager's position (Katz and Kahn, 1978). Specifically, they distinguish three basic levels: (1) top executives, (2) middle managers, and (3) first-level supervisors. Each level, according to Katz and Kahn, has its own unique leadership responsibilities. The top echelons are responsible primarily for determining the over-all mission of the firm and for generating grand strategy; the middle echelons, for interpreting and implementing mission and strategy; and the supervisory echelons, for administering the work itself.

If Katz and Kahn are correct, then we should expect significant differences in communication responsibilities among the three levels—since leadership is so closely bound up with communication behavior. Katz and Kahn propose three different leadership (hence, communication) styles: "charisma" for the top level, "human relations" for the middle level, and "equity" for the lower level.

Thus, the important question arises: Is it sensible to propose a single set of managerial communication responsibilities for all three levels of management?

A Recommended Answer

Although the Katz-Kahn position contains much wisdom, other authorities have identified serious flaws in it. Mintzberg (1973, pp. 110-113), for example, cites empirical evidence showing that even the first-level supervisor deals with strategic or structural changes *"in his own unit,"* and that "managers at all levels perform [all the] common roles, but with different emphasis." We can probably agree with Katz and Kahn that, say, the CEO of General Motors and a foreman on the GM assembly line will find themselves compelled to adopt different actions and different communication behaviors. And no doubt some managerial communication responsibilities will be more salient for the CEO, others for the foreman. But the position recommended here will be this: Despite differences in emphasis, there exists a hard core of communication responsibilities applicable (with variations) across the board to virtually all managers at all levels. These communication responsibilities are summarized in the checklist that follows.

Checklist of Communication Responsibilities

1. *To articulate goals and to encourage understanding of these goals.*[3] Goals embrace not only the overarching mission of the company as a whole, but also the objectives of the various subunits, such as departments or divisions. Goals also may be either short-term or long-term. A useful way of analyzing organizational goals is in terms of three basic functions, each of which must be satisfied at some minimal level if the firm is to survive at all (Redding, 1964, p. 43):

- The *task* function (the need to accomplish the prime purpose—providing goods or services to society—that justifies the company's existence).
- The *maintenance* function (the need to maintain the organization as a going concern, as an entity *per se*). This need is instrumental to the first, although many organizations reach a stage at which the maintenance function becomes an end in itself, and the task function almost fades away.
- The *human* function (the need to create conditions in which all members of the organization utilize their talents, realize their potential as human beings, and achieve as high a level of satisfaction as possible).

---

[3]This first communication responsibility does *not* assume that all the goals and subgoals within a company are necessarily congruent. It is common knowledge that complex organizations are characterized by many goal conflicts among various segments. A later chapter will examine this phenomenon.

2. *To disseminate (or supervise the dissemination of) information required for the daily operations of the company.* This includes not only the more obvious kinds of information—such as instructions, rules, and regulations—but also explanations of matters like the following: the relationship (if any!) between quality of performance and rewards (pay, promotion, and the like), the criteria determining rewards and penalties, problems facing the company (such as the competition), long-range plans, acquisitions, new products, and so on.

3. *To obtain, store, and retrieve information.* The following are especially vital:

- Obtaining the inputs required for informed decision making.
- Securing "organizational intelligence" (Wilensky, 1967). This includes finding out what's really going on in the company, and the degree to which managers and employees are implementing corporate goals (see especially Deal and Kennedy [1982] and Kaufman [1973]).
- Designing the basic structure of a computer-based management information system (MIS).
- Facilitating continuity by maintaining records ("organizational memory") so that new managers do not have to start from scratch.

Obviously, all the varied techniques associated with upward communication belong here.

4. *To coordinate the activities of individuals and units.* The basic theme here is to ensure that actions taken in one part of the organization are congruent with those taken in other parts. The most familiar (among many) devices are staff meetings, minutes of meetings, and reports.

5. *To receive and transmit information regarding the performance of subordinates; and, as needed, to take corrective action.* Even in companies dedicated to participative or Theory Y management styles, this responsibility must be met in some fashion. Included here then, are not only the traditional performance review (appraisal) conference but also variants of the peer review.

6. *To resolve destructive conflict, to negotiate, to conciliate.* (Note the qualifier: destructive, not constructive, conflict.) Fulfilling this responsibility requires such personal communication skills as empathic listening, persuasion (especially the gentler forms in "off-the-record" settings), advocacy, bargaining, and a sophisticated appreciation of the legitimate uses of ambiguity.

7. *To represent oneself, one's unit, or one's company in situations requiring explanation and advocacy.* Although the physical setting and audience will differ, essentially the same communication skills are involved whether the manager is dealing with his or her boss, another unit in the company, or an outside situation. Also, this seventh responsi-

bility applies to those numerous occasions when a manager finds it appropriate to defend decisions, explain policies, or advocate new proposals with subordinates. (When mass media presentations are necessary—such as in company newspapers or on closed-circuit TV—the manager will generally be well advised to call upon specialists for advice.) Some of the same communication skills apply here as in Item 6, above. The important difference, however, is that Item 6 refers to situations in which *destructive conflict* is occurring, or is threatened. That is not the case here.

8. *To help make the workplace a more satisfying and fulfilling—rather than alienating—experience for everyone in the organization who comes within one's sphere of influence.* Let there be no misunderstanding. Item 8 is not meant to embody the simple-minded notion that a business firm is a playground. The "happy worker is a productive worker" myth evaporated long ago, in the cold light of experience. Happiness, as such, is not the issue. The point is that, unless driven by sheer necessity, people simply will not take jobs, or remain in jobs, with organizations that make them feel like neglected cogs in an impersonal machine. The use of such feedback methods as sensing sessions, question-and-answer programs, and morale surveys is a prerequisite condition for accomplishing this eighth objective. Most important? Empathic listening.

9. *To foster the full utilization of human resources.* Obviously, meeting this responsibility entails a wide range of communication skills and techniques. It is also closely related to the overarching managerial philosophy that determines, in the last analysis, how the company is run. The "human resources" point of view, with its implications for managerial communication, will be examined in a later chapter.[4] For now, note some of the numerous communication means-to-ends:

- Training, coaching, counseling of subordinates—including goal-setting and MBO conferences.
- Internal recruiting—including job-posting systems.
- Participative decision making (PDM)—*authentic* PDM, not tokenism.
- Prompt and accurate feedback for subordinates on their job performance—both recognition of good work and candid identification of problems.

10. *To facilitate innovation.* To be sure, the degree of innovativeness, and the rapidity with which innovations are adopted, will vary according to the nature of the business. Some firms, like those in high

---

[4]Interested readers will find excellent summaries of human resources management and participative decision making in Kanter (1982), Miles and Rosenberg (1982), and Skinner (1981).

technology and pharmaceuticals, can almost say that innovation is their business. Others, like many assembly-line industries, require more stability. However, regardless of what a company does, stagnation is a constant threat. There seems to be a universal tendency for organizations to slip into the comfortable warmth of bureaucratic lethargy. Admittedly, encouraging innovation, or any kind of creativity, can be a high-risk occupation in many organizations—risky enough to have cost some venturesome souls their jobs. Meeting this tenth responsibility may require an even higher order of moral courage than of communication finesse.

Pending further discussion of this topic in later pages, we should note that organizational structure, entirely aside from the behavior of individual managers, exerts great influence upon the level of tolerance shown toward innovative ideas. Jay Galbraith (1982) argued that, in many cases, a separate and semiautonomous "innovating organization" must be established, parallel to the conventional "operating organization." Dunning and Sincoff (1980), applying sophisticated mathematical analysis, concluded that in any organization with four or more hierarchical levels, "unusually good ideas" tend to come in second-best to "ordinary ideas."

HOW ABOUT LOYALTY AND PRODUCTIVITY?

Have we somehow forgotten about two objectives sometimes proposed as prime goals of corporate communication: loyalty and productivity? These terms are about as controversial as apple pie and motherhood. All managements strive for a loyal work force, and all managements properly seek ways of improving productivity. However, pitfalls lurk in these innocent-sounding words.

Loyalty

Loyalty is a tricky concept. First, it should not be an end in itself. Loyalty is a means to an end—the end of achieving corporate effectiveness. Does any business firm have the moral right to ask its employees to be loyal to it, just for the sake of being loyal? The thoughtful answer is "no." Moreover, loyalty can actually be harmful to an organization when it is equated with the attitude "keep your mouth shut, no matter what." This is the misguided loyalty that makes nasty headlines about companies that finally get caught in a variety of mistakes and misdeeds. Finally, many managements fall into the attractive blunder of "preaching." But preaching is a form of condescension, which alienates most employees. (See the discussion of insensitivity in Chapter 6.)

Productivity

To postulate productivity as a separate communication responsibility is to create the misleading impression that none of the other responsibilities is relevant to improving productivity. The fact is that all ten communication responsibilities pertain to productivity. Furthermore, as with loyalty, trumpeting "better productivity" as a corporate objective frequently traps managements into preaching. When that happens, the implicit message as interpreted by employees is that only they—never managers—are the slackers. As surveys have repeatedly shown, many employees translate high-pressure productivity slogans into "speed up" (go back to Chapter 3 and review the conveyor-belt fallacy).

We could end this chapter in no better way than by taking to heart some wise words uttered by a veteran manager of corporate communication—Roger D'Aprix (formerly at Xerox). He warns managers that a formal communication program that emphasizes exhortation "won't motivate anyone. It won't make anyone more productive. It won't increase their loyalty" (D'Aprix, 1977, p. 185). Loyalty and productivity, argues D'Aprix, "would be much better served *if* people truly understood the meaning of their lives and *if* from that meaning they were able to foster a personal sense of hope for the future" (p. 170). The key term here is *meaning*. It encapsulates what D'Aprix urges as "the real mission" of all corporate communication: helping people to "understand the *meaning* of their lives in the work place" (1977, pp. 175, 170).

After reading this chapter and taking note of the wide range of attitudes and skills that the term *communication* can denote, managers may understandably feel a bit intimidated. But the next chapter should be reassuring. It shows that the task of managing the manager's communication is . . . well, manageable.

References

Barnard, Chester I. *The Functions of the Executive.* Cambridge, Mass.: Harvard University Press, 1938; 30th anniversary ed., 1968.

Beckhard, Richard. "The Confrontation Meeting." *Harvard Business Review* 45, no. 2 (March-April 1967): 149-55.

Coyle, Lee. "RSVP: The Ohio Bell Approach." *Public Relations Journal* 37, no. 2 (February 1981): 24-26.

D'Aprix, Roger M. *The Believable Corporation.* New York: Amacom, 1977.

Davis, Tim R. V. and Fred Luthans. "Managers in Action: A New Look at Their Behavior and Operating Modes." *Organizational Dynamics* 9, no. 1 (Summer 1980): 64-80.

Deal, Terrence E. and Allan A. Kennedy. *Corporate Cultures—the Rites and Rituals of Corporate Life.* Reading, Mass.: Addison-Wesley, 1982.

Downs, Anthony. *Inside Bureaucracy.* Boston: Little, Brown, 1967.

Dunning, Robert Scott and Michael Z. Sincoff. "Probability of Idea Acceptance in a Technologically Oriented Social Structure." *Technological Forecasting and Social Change* 18 (1980): 113-28.

Galbraith, Jay R. "Designing the Innovating Organization." *Organizational Dynamics* 10, no. 3 (Winter 1982): 5-25.

Galbraith, John Kenneth. *A Life in Our Times: Memoirs.* Boston: Houghton Mifflin, 1981.

Georgiades, Nicholas J. and Vanja Orlans. "The Supervision of Working Groups." In Michael Argyle, ed., *Social Skills and Work.* London and New York: Methuen, 1981, pp. 116-43.

Goodman, Ronald and Richard S. Ruch. "In the Image of the CEO." *Public Relations Journal* 37, no. 2 (February 1981): 14-19.

Gulick, Luther. "Notes on the Theory of Organizations." In L. Gulick and L. F. Urwick, eds., *Papers on the Science of Administration.* New York: Institute of Public Administration, Columbia University, 1937, pp. 3-45.

Kanter, Rosabeth Moss. "Dilemmas of Managing Participation." *Organizational Dynamics* 11, no. 1 (Summer 1982): 5-27.

Katz, Daniel and Robert L. Kahn. *The Social Psychology of Organizations,* 2d ed. New York: Wiley, 1978.

Kaufman, Herbert. *Administrative Feedback—Monitoring Subordinates' Behavior.* Washington, D.C.: Brookings Institution, 1973.

Lesly, Philip. *How We Discommunicate.* New York: Amacom, 1979.

Miles, Raymond E. and Howard R. Rosenberg. "The Human Resources Approach to Management: Second-Generation Issues." *Organizational Dynamics* 10, no. 3 (Winter 1982): 26-41.

Mintzberg, Henry. *The Nature of Managerial Work.* New York: Harper & Row, 1973.

Mintzberg, Henry. "The Manager's Job: Folklore and Fact." *Harvard Business Review* 53, no. 4 (July-August 1975): 49-61.

Redding, W. Charles. "The Organizational Communicator." In W. C. Redding and G. A. Sanborn, eds., *Business and Industrial Communication: A Source Book.* New York: Harper & Row, 1964, pp. 29-58.

Redfield, Charles E. *Communication in Management,* rev. ed. Chicago: University of Chicago Press, 1958; first ed., 1953.

Sayles, Leonard. *Managerial Behavior: Administration in Complex Organizations.* New York: McGraw-Hill, 1964.

Skinner, Wickham. "Big Hat, No Cattle: Managing Human Resources." *Harvard Business Review* 59, no. 4 (September-October 1981): 106-14.

Smircich, Linda and Gareth Morgan. "Leadership: The Management of Meaning." *Journal of Applied Behavioral Science* 18 (1982): 257-73.

Stewart, Rosemary. *Managers and Their Jobs.* London: Macmillan, 1967.

Travers, Robert M. W. *Man's Information System.* Scranton, Pa.: Chandler, 1970.

Wilensky, Harold. *Organizational Intelligence.* New York: Basic Books, 1967.

Zuegner, Charles. "The Communication Program: What Is It, What Does It Do?" *Journal of Organizational Communication,* 1980, no. 3, pp. 3-8.

CHAPTER 5

The Hallmarks of Excellence

The main difference between the Japanese and American industrial systems... is that Japanese managers communicate and American executives do not.

Louis C. Williams, Vice-President, Hill and Knowlton, Inc., in the Journal of Organizational Communication, *no. 3, 1981, p. 19.*

Americans are not only the richest people in the world, they're the best educated and best informed. There is ... "a shortage of morons." Yet our communications still tend to be patronizing, condescending and simplistic.

James W. Davant, Chairman and Chief Executive Officer, Paine Webber, Inc., in the New York Times, *Nov. 30, 1977, p. A-25.*

The prevailing view is that business treats people like so many statistics, to be manipulated in the same way that engineering data are run through a computer.

Arnold R. Deutsch, Chairman, Deutsch, Shea & Evans, Inc., in The Human Resources Revolution *(New York: McGraw-Hill, 1979), p. 28.*

I am concerned about how rarely North American top managements are truly honest in their communication .... In this era of transactional analysis, EST and hot tubs, we've become masters of camouflage .... We say maybe, or sometimes even yes, when we mean no.

R. M. Clarke, President, Celanese Specialty Operations, quoted in the Journal of Communication Management, *no. 4, 1982, p. 17.*

> DOUBLE TALK GRIPS BUSINESS REPORTS AS FIRMS TRY TO SUGARCOAT BAD NEWS.
>
> *Headline from news story by Thomas Petzinger Jr., Wall Street Journal, March 31, 1982, p. 25.*
>
> Reading a house organ is like going down in warm maple syrup for the third time.
>
> *Robert Townsend, former Chairman of the Board, Avis Rent-a-Car Corporation, in Up the Organization (New York: Knopf, 1970), p. 126.*
>
> When people sense themselves to be viewed as jackasses, they will ... resist hearing management's messages, no matter how clear the type or how pretty the pictures.
>
> *Harry Levinson, President, Levinson Institute; Thomas Henry Carroll/Ford Foundation Distinguished Professor of Business Administration, Harvard University, in The Great Jackass Fallacy (Boston: Graduate School of Business Administration, Harvard University, 1973), p. 11.*
>
> Opinion Research Corporation [Princeton, New Jersey] reports that today, 69 percent of middle managers complain ... of too many decisions made at the top that were made by them a year ago. And 70 percent of all workers believe top management has lost touch with the rank and file.
>
> *News story in Family Weekly, January 30, 1983, p. 3.*
>
> Only about one-half of all survey respondents describe communication in their organizations as candid and accurate. More than two-thirds believe that official communication doesn't tell the full story.
>
> *Report of findings from 1982 survey of 32,000 employees in 26 U.S. and Canadian organizations (conducted by IABC and Towers, Perrin, Forster & Crosby) in Foehrenbach and Rosenberg, 1982, p. 7.*

Are these depressing quotations the fruits of a biased search to provide a litany for self-flagellation? On the contrary, they could be multiplied many times over. No reader is compelled to agree with them. But they represent in every case either the sober judgment of qualified observers or the empirical evidence derived from scientifically-competent surveys.

The problems identified in these quotations are especially pertinent to the issues dealt with in this and the next chapter.

HOW MANY MANAGERS CAN WALK ON WATER?

The perfect manager—the manager who can walk on water—is an abstraction never to be encountered in real life. But whenever we set out to improve ourselves, we have in mind an ideal—even though we know the ideal is unattainable. And so, in this and succeeding chapters, we shall be talking about ideal managerial communicators. Only after we clearly envision what we should work *toward* can we know what we should work *on*. Thus, we find ourselves at Step 4 of the nine-step schedule: taking aim (see Chapter 2).

Six all-inclusive characteristics will be proposed as descriptors of the "ideal managerial communicator." As you will see, each represents a broad range of skills and competencies. We shall be calling these the *hallmarks of excellence*—they are the hallmarks, or criteria, by which we recognize the ideal. They answer the question: "Were we ever to encounter such a noble creature, what would the ideal managerial communicator be like?"

The present chapter will discuss the first four hallmarks: self-worth, integrity, wisdom, and credibility. Succeeding chapters will address the other two: sensitivity and imagination.

THE FIRST THREE HALLMARKS: THE PRIMARY REQUISITES OF GOOD MANAGERIAL COMMUNICATION

The first three hallmarks—self-worth, integrity, and wisdom—are considered as a group because they constitute an interrelated set of characteristics that pervade all managerial communication, regardless of circumstances. For the present we shall focus upon that aspect of communication described in the preceding chapter as the personal domain. The reason for this is that all managers are individual, unique persons before they ever become managers. The first three hallmarks, then, represent *basic personality attributes*, attributes that have a profound influence on all our communication behavior.

Unless a manager demonstrates that he or she possesses a minimum of certain personality characteristics commonly esteemed in our culture, no amount of effort expended on improving communication skills will pay off. On the other hand, any manager displaying these attributes—even if he or she may not be regarded as a polished speaker or writer—enjoys a high probability of being perceived as a reasonably effective communicator.

We need not take a stand on the intricate complexities of trait versus situational versus interactional theories of personality (the subject of long-standing controversies among social scientists) to agree that dominant individuals, whether heroes or villains, have made or broken companies by the sheer force of their personalities. We can call to mind Henry Ford, John D. Rockefeller, Andrew Carnegie, Alfred Sloan, Harold

Geneen, William C. Durant, William Agee, and John DeLorean. On a less global scale, any adult of mature age who has been employed for a few years can bear witness to instances in which an executive, a superintendent, or a foreman has "turned things around" (for better or worse).

No argument is being made here to support a "great man" (or "great woman") theory of corporate leadership. Social scientists long ago demonstrated the importance of situational determinants of leaders' actions. But the scientific evidence can never justify our denying the potential impact of the unique human personality. As managers interact, hour by hour and day by day, with subordinates, superiors, peers, and others, a fundamental source (though not the only source) of their behavior will always be certain attributes that characterize their unique personalities.

This remains true even when we accept the irrefutable fact that most of the important decisions, particularly in large corporations, are made by groups rather than by isolated individuals. The concept of the *technostructure*, first articulated by John Kenneth Galbraith, has now earned general acceptance among both academic theorists and practicing managers. It is neatly epitomized in this passage (Galbraith, 1967, p. 69): "nearly all powers—initiation, character of development, rejection or acceptance—are exercised deep in the company. It is not the managers who decide. Effective decision is lodged deeply in the technical, planning and other specialized staff."

Peter F. Drucker, who has been called the most influential adviser to corporate managements living in the last half of the century, agrees that corporate leadership is a collective, rather than an individual, phenomenon: "*individually* a manager is just another fellow employee.... It is therefore inappropriate to speak of managers as leaders. They are 'members of the leadership group,'" (Drucker, 1974, p. 369).

But whether we prefer to consider the typical manager as a charismatic leader or as just another employee, that same manager exerts influence upon others (and is influenced by others) as an individual person. As D'Aprix reminds us, "The kingpin of any employee communication effort is the common, garden-variety manager" (1977, p. 40). To the average employee, the manager *is* the company. The managers are the ones who "interpret and enforce the rules, evaluate performance, pass out the rewards and the punishments" (D'Aprix, 1977, p. 40). And so we pose the question: Can we identify the basic personality attributes that characterize the best managerial communicators? The answer is a provisional yes.

A central core of communicator attributes represents an area of agreement apparently shared by large numbers of theorists, researchers, and practitioners. The agreement is in substance rather than in terminology—terminology varies from writer to writer. What follows is my interpretation of this central core.

EXHIBIT 5.1 The First Three Hallmarks of Excellence

DESCRIPTIVE TERMS USED WHEN MANAGER IS PERCEIVED AS:

	Having the Proper Amount	Deficient	Having Too Much
1. Self-worth (Reality-based acceptance of self as worthy person)	confident having inner strength poised sane secure having self-respect	apologetic Caspar Milquetoast defensive indecisive insecure paranoid thin-skinned wishy-washy	arrogant ruthless closed-minded self-satisfied conceited smug condescending superior dogmatic high and mighty overbearing patronizing
2. Integrity (Adherence to ethical and moral standards)	ethical honest honorable moral reliable responsible trustworthy	a con artist a cut-throat an empire-builder immoral Machiavellian manipulative an operator selfish a sly fox a wheeler-dealer	*Not applicable* (How is it possible to have too much integrity?)
3. Wisdom (Depth of insight; ability to see relationships; broad view)	far-sighted having perspective reasonable sensible sophisticated thoughtful	unable to see the forest for the trees naive near-sighted pedantic having a rule-book mind shallow shortsighted superficial	*Not applicable* (How is it possible to have too much wisdom?)

Examine Exhibit 5.1. Here you will find a summary of the essential components of the first three hallmarks. In the left-hand column each hallmark—which is to say each personal attribute of the "ideal" communicator—is identified by a concise label: *self-worth, integrity, wisdom*. The second, third, and fourth columns contain examples of the descriptive terms (adjectives, nouns, phrases) frequently heard when people speak of individual managers whom they *perceive* as possessing—or not possessing—each of the three attributes. Thus, if Jane Doe consistently impresses you as a person with an inflated opinion of herself, you may describe her in terms like *arrogant* or *smug*.

The sequence of attributes is not random. A set of logical priorities governs the ordering of the three hallmarks: self-worth comes first, on the grounds that it is a precondition for the others. That is, until a person achieves at least a minimally realistic acceptance of himself or herself as being worthy of respect, it seems improbable that that person can act either morally or wisely. In like manner, if, our backs to the wall, we were forced to make such an unhappy choice, we would probably "prefer to work with forthright plodders rather than with devious geniuses" (in the words of Vice-Admiral James B. Stockdale [1982, p. 207]).

Self-Worth

The concept of *self-worth* presented here is modeled closely upon the recent research of Glauser (1981), who not only developed a questionnaire to measure it but also carried out an elaborate experiment in which he examined the actual oral communication behavior of persons with high and with low scores. Combining self-worth scores with scores on a "verbal dominance" scale (measuring the degree to which a person dominates a conversation), Glauser created thirty-seven pairs of college students representing the four possible combinations of high self-worth, low self-worth, high dominance, and low dominance. Each pair then worked for thirty minutes on an open-ended decision-making task, in which they had to reach agreement.

He then content-analyzed the conversations, secured various self-ratings and evaluations of partners, and looked to see whether there were consistent differences in the ways the four types of individuals communicated. Such differences did indeed emerge. Most significant for present purposes is his conclusion that "those high in both self-worth and verbal dominance . . . were perceived as more open and relaxed by their partners, were highly satisfied with the interactions, experienced low levels of tension, and were rated high in social attraction and task attraction" (Glauser, 1981, p. xii).

I am defining self-worth here as does Glauser: "a general, evaluative attitude toward the self, which encompasses the individual's feelings of personal worth, usefulness, liking for self, and ability to make contributions to the lives of others" (p. 20).

Integrity

The intended meaning of *integrity* is probably obvious. It denotes the degree to which a manager is perceived as measuring up to whatever ethical/moral standards the *observer* holds to be relevant in a particular situation. Note the italicized word, *observer*. This means that if a manager subscribes to a code of ethics sharply at variance with an observer's code, he or she will simply have to live with the fact that communication with that observer is unlikely to be effective (since the alternative—capitulating to the other's code of ethics—would be an unacceptable violation of one's own code!).

Quoting Admiral Stockdale again (1982, pp. 206–207): "Integrity is one of those words which many people keep in that desk drawer labeled 'too hard.' . . . You can't buy or sell it." Nevertheless, the admiral is no doubt correct when he asserts that, in the typical organizational hierarchy where "people's fates are decided by committees or boards," those who come across (rightly or wrongly) as deficient in integrity "are dead." Can you imagine yourself being positively influenced by a managerial communicator whom you regard as dishonest, or conniving, or vicious?

In his provocative chapter on managerial ethics, Drucker declares that the main desideratum is "plain, everyday honesty. Businessmen, we are told solemnly, should not cheat, steal, lie, bribe, or take bribes. But nor should anyone else." Then, he rightly concludes: "there neither is a separate ethics of business, nor is one needed" (Drucker, 1974, p. 366).

Wisdom

By now you may be comparing these first three hallmarks of communication excellence to apple pie and motherhood: be aware of your own worth, be ethical, and be wise! Well, even though all this may indeed have the ring of banality, the fact remains—as numerous survey studies have demonstrated—that there is abroad in the land a widespread tendency to doubt the universal correctness of decision making on the part of management in major corporations.

For example, in their surveys of thousands of employees in General Motors and AT&T, Goodman and Ruch (1981) offer more documentation, if such were needed, that employees' image of top management depends crucially upon their belief that senior managers are really competent decision makers (translation: that they demonstrate wisdom). Even in management-oriented publications, articles and editorials appear regularly featuring the theme that grave errors in managerial judgment (wisdom) are largely responsible for the beatings visited upon U.S. industries by Japanese and other foreign competitors. Item: in 1980 the *Harvard Business Review* published an article with the provocative title "Managing Our Way to Economic Decline" (Hayes and Abernathy, 1980). The publishers were deluged under hundreds of thousands of requests for reprints. Item: in 1983 the *Wall Street Journal* published an essay on the troubles of the steel industry, under the headline "Steel's Management Has Itself to Blame." The writer defended the thesis that "poor decisions, particularly in capital spending, bear as much responsibility . . . as do high wages and benefits" (O'Boyle, 1983).

A common criticism of managerial decision making is that it is too preoccupied with short-term results, rather than long-term planning. A corollary is that too many top executives lack the perspective to separate what should be high-priority concerns from immediate and superficial considerations. All this bears upon what is meant here by *wisdom*. Wisdom, although it depends upon knowledge, is much more than knowledge. It involves the ability to see resemblances among dissimilar things and differences among similar things. It is judgment, rather than the mere mastery of facts. In Davis's words, "Knowledge is accumulated in discrete bits; wisdom is not divisible. . . . Because knowledge is incremental, it is measurable; wisdom is not" (1982, p. 77).

The point of all this is that a manager's communication skills cannot be separated from the kind of person he or she is—or is believed to be. And most decisive of all personal attributes, in their influence upon a manager's ways of communicating, are those represented by the first three hallmarks of excellence: self-worth, integrity, and wisdom.

CAN THE AVERAGE MANAGER DO ANYTHING ABOUT THESE BASIC ATTRIBUTES?

Since the present chapter aims to deal with objectives or criteria, rather than with specific improvement techniques, this important question will receive only a brief answer here. More will be said later.

The briefest answer is in the affirmative. Yes, even basic personal attributes are subject to change, albeit within limits. And I am not referring to psychiatric intervention! An individual manager can first—preferably with help from others—conduct a thorough self-assessment, especially in the area of identifying underlying assumptions, as discussed in Chapter 3.

But in addition to doing that, managers would be well advised to identify the constraints placed upon them by various corporate pressures, especially the reward system and the power structure. As many of the severest critics of modern management have conceded, inappropriate reward systems account for much that is questionable in managerial behavior. For example, in the United States the most salient rewards—sometimes amounting to commandments—induce corporate managements to become obsessed with "the bottom line" in short-range terms (such as quarterly earnings reports). But the rewards for sophisticated, long-range planning—always plagued by uncertainties, ambiguities, and risks—are frequently hard to discern.

Besides the reward system in the company (the *real* reward system, not necessarily the one loudly proclaimed), the manager should also consider the power structure. In her *Harvard Business Review* article, now become famous, Rosabeth Moss Kanter (1979) makes the distinction between "oppressive" and "productive" uses of managerial power. The former—characterized by pettiness, harrassment, and rule-book pedantry—is a natural outcome, Kanter claims, of occupying dead-end, no-clout jobs. As we shall see in a later chapter, she urges that managements give their closest attention to restructuring positions in the company so as to eliminate as many of these jobs as possible.

Thus, to effect improvement in basic personal attributes, managers must take into account not only their individual psyches but the total corporate environments in which they live. Admittedly this raises a broader issue: To what degree is any manager really free to be himself or herself?

THE MANAGER IN PERSPECTIVE: FORCES AND CONSTRAINTS EXERTING IMPACT UPON A MANAGER'S BEHAVIOR

Look at Exhibit 5.2. It is relevant not only to the present discussion but to everything in the book. Direct your attention first to the two large boxes. The upper one represents the manager and his or her ways of managing and communicating. The lower one represents organizational outcomes—such things as productivity (whether in terms of goods or services), profitability, public acceptance or support, and the like. You will note that two arrows, pointing in opposite directions, connect these two boxes.

The arrows are no more than a graphic device for reminding us that any causal connections between managerial performance and organizational output are two-directional. That is, not only does a manager's behavior have an impact upon organizational outcomes, but organizational outcomes also have an impact upon the manager's behavior. This is a fact too often neglected. For example, common sense tells us that any supervisor is likely to be a more effective—and more humane—supervisor if his or her workers are highly capable people, turning out superior products at a rate above normal expectations. And managements of companies noted for their consistently high levels of productivity find it easier to practice better managerial methods than do managements of companies drowning in red ink. We always have to think in terms of two-way causality.

This issue of "the direction of causality between the behavior of the leader and the behavior of the follower" has been addressed only recently by organizational researchers (Katz and Kahn, 1978, pp. 562-65). But, as Katz and Kahn observe, to ask the question in terms of which came first, as with the chicken and the egg, is to pose the wrong

EXHIBIT 5.2 Forces and Constraints Exerting Impact upon a Manager's Behavior

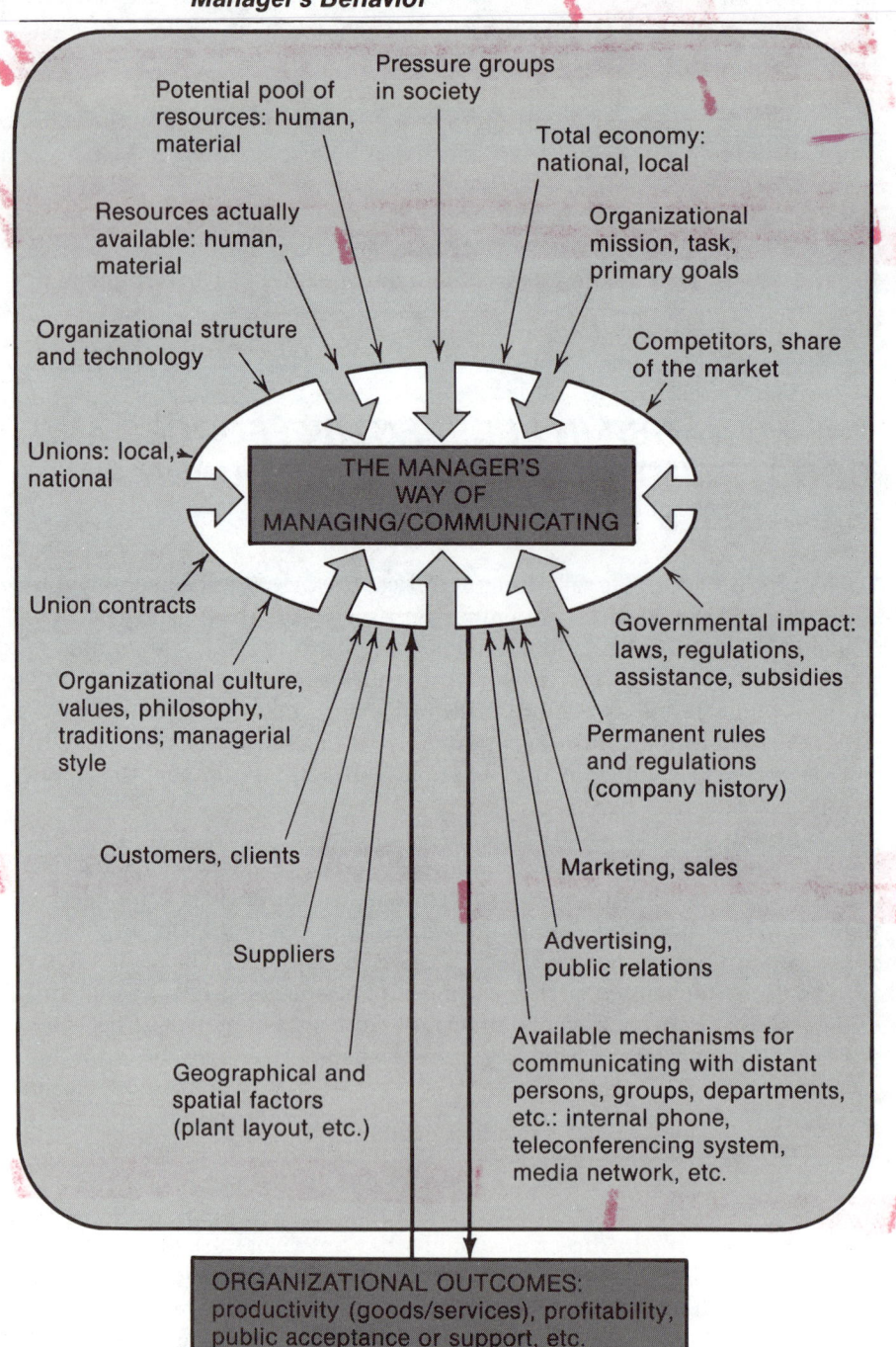

Forces pointing inward to **THE MANAGER'S WAY OF MANAGING/COMMUNICATING:**

- Potential pool of resources: human, material
- Pressure groups in society
- Total economy: national, local
- Resources actually available: human, material
- Organizational mission, task, primary goals
- Organizational structure and technology
- Competitors, share of the market
- Unions: local, national
- Union contracts
- Organizational culture, values, philosophy, traditions; managerial style
- Governmental impact: laws, regulations, assistance, subsidies
- Permanent rules and regulations (company history)
- Customers, clients
- Marketing, sales
- Suppliers
- Advertising, public relations
- Geographical and spatial factors (plant layout, etc.)
- Available mechanisms for communicating with distant persons, groups, departments, etc.: internal phone, teleconferencing system, media network, etc.

ORGANIZATIONAL OUTCOMES: productivity (goods/services), profitability, public acceptance or support, etc.

question. We are dealing with "mutually reinforcing processes"—hence, with a "*circular* pattern of causality" (p. 562; emphasis added).

In truth, two-directional arrows in Exhibit 5.2 could also be drawn to connect the organizational outcomes box with *all* the forces and constraints embodied in the various balloons, for all these factors impinge upon outcomes—entirely aside from the manager's behavior. Thus there is no intent here to suggest that the only force exerting direct impact upon corporate outcomes is managerial behavior. The typical manager is mediator as well as initiator.

To expand further upon all of this would go far beyond the purposes and limitations of the book. But the recommendation is that you come back to Exhibit 5.2 from time to time, as a reminder that any manager is "in large measure, the kind of communicator that the organization compels [him or her] to be. . . . the very fact of holding a position in an organization determines many of the ways in which a person speaks, listens, writes, and reads" (Redding, 1964, p. 29). (Note the qualifying phrase "in large measure.")

We next consider the fourth hallmark. It is discussed in the same chapter as the first three because—as will become evident—it is a logical consequence of self-worth, integrity, and wisdom. But now we move from underlying personality attributes to specific communication events and behaviors.

THE FOURTH HALLMARK: CREDIBILITY

The term *credibility gap,* despite having become a cliché during the 1970s, identifies one of the most critical and most pervasive causes of communication failure. A moment's reflection will confirm why this should be so. By definition, *credible* means believable. Is it likely that any person in possession of his or her senses would respond favorably to a message emanating from an "unbelievable" source?

The issue, of course, is not whether credibility enhances a communicator's effectiveness. Clearly, it does. Rather, the issue is this: What accounts for credibility? In other words, *why* is one source regarded as highly credible, while another is viewed as totally unreliable? Readers who have had occasion to plow through the recent research literature will confirm that "source credibility" accounts for an enormous share of the scholarly work in the field of human communication. Indeed, this topic may be the most thoroughly investigated of all topics in the field—just one review, covering only "major studies" between the years 1930 and 1969, included findings from no fewer than 110 empirical investigations (Littlejohn, 1971, pp. 1-40).

Since this is a guidebook and not a treatise, we must be selective—

and even arbitrary—in attempting to distill a compact set of practical conclusions from such a vast reservoir of material. Remember, then, that much more can be said than what is said here. Several assertions need to be made.

1. *In a special sense, credibility does not exist.* Credibility is not some sort of entity that belongs to or inheres in a message source. Rather, credibility is an *attributed quality*—attributed in all cases by a specified observer (perceiver). President Doe of the XYZ Corporation does not possess credibility. Whatever credibility he "has" lies in the eyes of the beholders— those of us who listen to him speak or read his words. This is a crucial fact to remember. Forgetting it can set us off on a wild-goose chase by diverting our attention from the crux of the matter: that the intersection of relationships among message source, subject matter of message, and message receiver combines to determine an attribution of credibility.

2. Even as an attributed quality, *credibility is not a constant.* A communicator may be regarded as credible when speaking on Topic A, in Situation B, to Audience C. But the same communicator may be regarded as low in credibility when speaking on Topic B, even to the same audience. For example, a few years ago I directed a large-scale survey project, of which a major portion focused upon a comparison of credibility ratings assigned by corporate employees to company publications versus union publications. Without going into details, I can report one unequivocal finding: When the subject matter of news stories had to do with company matters, employees (including union members) consistently rated the credibility of company publications higher than that of the union publications. However, when the subject matter had to do with union affairs or with political and economic issues, just the reverse was the case. In the eyes of employees, then, management credibility varied with the message content: in one case, it was high; in the other, low. Therefore, it would have been misleading to inquire about, or to discuss, a single entity called "management credibility."

3. *Authority is not necessarily associated with credibility.* No manager's credibility is automatic merely by virtue of the fact that he or she is a manager. Regrettably, many managers fail to realize this. They too often assume *ipse dixit:* I have spoken, therefore I am believed. The truth is that, in many instances (depending upon message content and message receivers), being a manager is a downright liability so far as

credibility is concerned. For example, Richetto (1969) conducted an in-depth investigation of supervisors' credibility (as rated by their subordinates) in the Marshall Space Flight Center (NASA) at Huntsville, Alabama. He collected data from 178 nonsupervisory employees working in two research laboratories. One of his prime objectives was to discover whether supervisors or nonsupervisors (fellow employees) were the preferred sources of information. Richetto identified three disparate kinds of message content ("topic areas"):
a. *Task*—job-related information.
b. *Political*—information regarding internal politics, such as promotions and demotions, power struggles, and the like.
c. *Social-emotional*—personal problems not directly related to the job including informal counseling.

The findings were quite dramatic. Even in the task area, where the conventional wisdom would lead us to expect that most subordinates would rank their immediate supervisors at the top, only about half (52 percent, to be exact) of the respondents reported supervisors to be their preferred sources. In the other two topic areas, preferences for supervisors were found among only small minorities: in the political area, only 6 percent; and in the social-emotional area, only 11 percent (Richetto, 1969, pp. 93–101; Redding, 1972, pp. 301–305). These data, of course, come from only one research study. However, informal evidence suggests that they are not atypical.

The Dimensions of Credibility

Even though, as was pointed out in Item 1 above, credibility is not an object that we can transport from person to person, it is a quality attributed to a communicator by observers. There are, therefore, two sets of parties always involved when we consider credibility: the focal person (or persons) and the evaluator (or evaluators).

When we think of credibility, we almost always have in mind the credibility of *message senders*—speakers, writers, mass media, and so on. However, a fact frequently neglected is that message senders may, in a sense, also evaluate the credibility of *message receivers*. You may ask, "Credibility of message receivers? Does that make sense?" Yes, it does, and especially in the corporate context. Think of the manager who distrusts another person. A manager may, for example, hesitate to disclose certain information to a boss, or to another manager, or to a subordinate. Why? Because the manager believes that the receiver "wouldn't understand what I'm talking about," "can't be trusted to keep this confidential," or the like. We can think of this as an assessment of the receiver's credibility.

Now let us get to the heart of the matter: What are the factors that cause us to regard a person (or a medium, such as a corporate publication) as credible or not credible? This question has kept numerous researchers busy over several decades. Until rather recently, the great majority of them dedicated themselves to a search for the Holy Grail—a set of factors that people everywhere use in making evaluations of credibility. The assumption was that these factors were universals, valid under all possible communication conditions.

Now, after a decade or more of further research and spirited debate, the contest over whether or not such universals exist is a kind of draw. On the one hand, there is general agreement that a *very few* determinants do seem to operate in virtually all communication situations. But, on the other hand, there is also agreement that various special factors become important according to the nature of the situation.[1]

A couple of years ago I had occasion to propose to a group of managers a synthesis (if such were possible) of universal—or almost universal—determinants of credibility, drawn from what appeared to be the most influential theoretical and scientific sources. For present purposes, there emerged from this effort a set of three factors, which are described in Exhibit 5.3.

These factors, interestingly enough, closely parallel the three components of credibility originally identified by Aristotle in his *Rhetoric*, written in the fourth century BC and still influential in the twentieth century AD. Aristotle argued—as do modern social scientists—that the most powerful single determinant of a speaker's effectiveness is character (*ethos*), as perceived by the audience. The three components of *ethos*, according to Aristotle, were good sense, good moral character, and goodwill. Look at Exhibit 5.3 and make the comparisons:

C—competence (compare Aristotle's good sense).
R—reliability (compare Aristotle's good moral character).
I—intentions—meaning good intentions toward the audience (compare Aristotle's goodwill).

The important point is that a manager's credibility will be high if he or she is perceived by others—subordinates, bosses, peers, and so on—as

---

[1] Readers endowed with both the curiosity and the time can get an idea of the problems and controversies on this topic by consulting, as starters: Giffin, 1967; Simons, Berkowitz, and Moyer, 1970; Applbaum and Anatol, 1972; Applbaum and Anatol, 1974; Cronkhite and Liska, 1976; Delia, 1976.

EXHIBIT 5.3 Credibility: Some Important Dimensions

The Most Universal Determinants
These are the basic criteria upon which evaluators base their judgments of the credibility of focal persons. Operative in the great majority of situations, they may be applied largely below the level of awareness.

- **C—Competence** Refers to focal person's know-how, good sense, intelligence, expertise, experience, skill, and so on—as perceived by evaluator
- **R—Reliability** Refers to apparent congruence between focal person's words and deeds; consistency between one utterance and another; honesty and sincerity; ethics; moral character—as perceived by evaluators
- **I—Intentions** Refers to inferences made by evaluators regarding focal person's attitudes and intentions toward the evaluators (or toward others whom the evaluators hold in high esteem); goodwill; concern for welfare of audience (or other evaluators)

Reasons (Factors) behind the Determinants
For example, we may ask why a listener evaluates a manager as competent. We may discover that the listener puts great store in the fact that the manager is a graduate of the college from which the listener graduated. Here are a few more examples of influential factors:
  General reputation (generalizations, including such stereotypes as "Never trust anyone over thirty," or "Money speaks.")
  Membership in same group (friendship group, college class, home town)
  Perceived power wielded by focal person
  Setting (formal versus informal)
  Authentication (official versus unofficial)

knowledgeable, trustworthy, and sincerely concerned with the welfare of those others.[2]

THE CRUCIAL IMPORTANCE OF MANAGEMENT CREDIBILITY

Everyday living has taught us that a *sine qua non* of successful person-to-person relationships is trust. And a moment's thought reminds us that trust and credibility are so closely related as to be almost interchangeable terms. Without trust—or credibility—friendships, business partnerships, and marriages collapse. And without credibility, corporate managers find it impossible to function.

---

[2]Experiment-based support for this conclusion can be found in such studies as those of Falcione (1974) and Richetto (1969). For a book-length discussion of credibility as it relates to the modern corporation, see D'Aprix (1977).

76 The Hallmarks of Excellence

Glance back at several of the quotations presented at the beginning of this chapter: the fourth says that much managerial communication is dishonest; the fifth reports corporate double talk as a means of sugarcoating bad news; the sixth describes house organs as tubs of warm maple syrup; and the last reports on a recent large-scale survey revealing that between one-half and two-thirds of the respondents perceived their employing organizations as deficient in candor, accuracy, or fairness. All these quotations are vivid reminders of an unpalatable truth: that large numbers of people lack faith in the credibility of many corporate managements.

Although we can easily understand the crucial role of credibility in the personal domain of managerial communication, let us direct our attention to the corporate domain. Keep in mind that, just like individual persons, impersonal institutions—corporations, newspapers, television networks, labor unions, government agencies—are also perceived as having high or low credibility. Thus, we hear remarks like these: "I don't believe a damned word that company says about unfair foreign competition—not since that lemon they conned me into buying last year!" or "Every government is run by liars and nothing they say should be believed" (assertion attributed to the famous iconoclastic journalist I. F. Stone).

Or take a couple of in-house testimonials:

> It seems to me that the honest, two-way communication I read about, issue after issue, in [name of corporate employee newspaper], just exists in words on paper and not in action.
>
> (Corporate employee writing to the company editor about company publications, especially those describing the performance appraisal system. Ragan Report, Sept. 15, 1975, p. 2.)
>
> It's damned difficult, for example, to tell your stockholders you never had it so good, your employees that things could be better, and the union that you're going broke—without some loss of credibility. But so help me, that's precisely what a lot of business communicators—usually at the urging of their management—have been trying to do for years.
>
> (Manager of internal communications for a major oil company, speaking at a conference of the International Association of Business Communicators, June 1971. IABC News, July 1971, p. 2.)

It is not uncommon for a perception of high or low credibility to be so overpowering as to produce a 180-degree shift in our opinions on important issues. William H. Whyte, Jr., recounted a little experiment years ago, an experiment now become famous: A CIO newspaper had carried a large cartoon chart, with the heading "The Four Goals of Labor." The experimenters pulled a dirty trick. They clipped the chart from the paper and reproduced it exactly as it was—with one important change. They added a line at the bottom reading, "From June 3 N. A. M. [National Association of Manufacturers] Newsletter." They then showed the chart to a group of twenty CIO members, asking them if they regarded the chart as "a fair presentation of labor's goals." Four said that it was, and two were not sure. But the other fourteen "damned it as 'patronizing,' 'loaded,' 'paternalistic,' 'makes me want to spit' . . ." (Whyte, 1952, p. 22).

> You may want to try this on yourself: A famous historical personage uttered these words: "[From] the possession of different degrees and kinds of property . . . ensues a division of the society into different interests and parties." Suppose I inform you that the speaker was Karl Marx. How credible do you find his words?[3]

That the credibility of a message source should exert such commanding force upon our judgment is not surprising. Nor is it evidence of human gullibility. From past experience we learn to what degree we can believe what a communicator tells us. In terms of objective "facts," our evaluations may be correct or incorrect; but it may require months or years of new experiences to shift an incorrect evaluation to a correct one. Companies with new managements have learned this painful fact. After years of hostilities and suspicions between, let us say, an old management and the union, the new management will encounter formidable obstacles in its efforts to convince workers that a new era has really dawned.

Ponder once more the 1982 IABC survey (cited earlier) indicating that at least half of 32,000 employees in twenty-six companies had serious doubts about the candor, accuracy, and fairness of corporate publications. Similar results had been obtained in the IABC survey of a year earlier, representing 45,000 employees in forty companies (Gildea, 1981). It may be no exaggeration to conclude that mediocre credibility could be the biggest single obstacle confronting management-employee communication in contemporary corporations.

Common Danger Signals of Low Credibility

What should managers be looking for when they start wondering about their credibility ratings, especially among subordinates and employees in general? Here are a few questions to consider:

---

[3]Actually the speaker was James Madison, writing in *The Federalist,* November 23, 1787. Does this knowledge modify your interpretation of the words? Do you find yourself saying, "Oh well, what this quotation *really* says is . . ."?

- On how many occasions in the past have deeds failed to follow words? How many rosy—or alarming—predictions have turned out to be false? (Were the predictions stated dogmatically, or were they carefully hedged?)
- How often has management played games with employees—for example, by concealing the true motives behind certain decisions (or even by propagating downright falsehoods)?
- To what extent do company publications restrict themselves to acting as a cheering section? Do they merit Townsend's epithet "warm maple syrup" by featuring nothing but picnics, anniversaries, and bowling scores?
- To what extent do management utterances consist of "inspirational" sermons on such themes as "pulling in our belts," "loyalty to the team," and the "work ethic"?
- How often is it easy for people to see contradictions between official pronouncements (policies, rules, regulations) on the one hand and everyday practices on the other? Why?
- Perhaps most important of all, the real litmus test: How is bad news handled? (Stonewalled? Distorted? Whitewashed?)

Keep in mind that most managers probably overestimate their credibility ratings with subordinates and employees. For example, in a research study conducted in a large manufacturing firm, Minter (1969) asked seven top executives—the president and six vice-presidents—to predict how most supervisory and managerial personnel (in two divisions) would respond to the question: "How do you feel this statement applies in this Company: *You can always trust management's word?*" Six of the seven predicted that the supervisors and managers would agree "overwhelmingly" that management's word could be trusted virtually 100 percent of the time. What did the supervisors and managers (representing three hierarchical levels) tell the researcher? Roughly half

---

EXHIBIT 5.4   A Frightening Example

The Knight newspaper chain conducted a survey in the Spring of 1970 in several major cities (such as Miami, Philadelphia, Detroit, and Washington) and in rural areas of North and South Carolina. The question dealt with the famous moon landing of July 20, 1969—almost a year earlier. Since the survey admittedly fell short of a scientific sampling of the population, no precise statistical findings were reported. However, "wide support" was registered for the "theory that the government and the news media conspired to hoodwink the public with a fake telecast"—probably produced somewhere in the Arizona desert! Had such a finding been a true picture of the entire adult population, the United States would have been ungovernable. *(Chicago Sun-Times,* June 15, 1970, p. 7)

---

the sample, when interviewed, reported that they would trust management's word only half the time or less. As he went up the hierarchical ladder, Minter found higher and higher levels of this false optimism on the part of managerial respondents (see Minter, 1969, vol. 4, pp. 792-93).

Suggestion: Conduct a Credibility Audit

Suppose that Manager Jane Doe speaks to her boss (Audience A) for the purpose of urging additions to her staff (Topic 1). Suppose also that she is interviewed for an article in the company newspaper, in which she defends the use of subcontractors for plant maintenance work (Audience B and Topic 2). In the first instance, it happens that her personal communication skills are especially critical; in the second, her corporate skills (see Chapter 4).

As common sense—as well as research findings—would suggest, Jane's credibility on the topic of increased staff, with her boss as audience, may be drastically different from her credibility on the topic of subcontracting, with an audience made up of the general work force. A credibility audit would induce Jane to analyze these different audience/topic combinations and, on the basis of such analysis, to design her presentations accordingly. A manager's credibility audit would include questions such as the following:

C *(competence)*—Have I done my homework on the subject? How can I demonstrate—to this specific audience—that I know what I'm talking about? To what extent will I be perceived as biased? Why? How can I counteract such a perception?

R *(reliability)*—Am I known as one whose deeds match my words? Have I been caught in contradictions, or even lies?

I *(intentions)*—What evidence have I produced, or what evidence can I introduce, to demonstrate that I have my listeners' best interests at heart? Have I been regarded as a manager who rides rough-shod over other people? Am I perceived as one who operates on the principle that "nice guys finish last?"

The credibility audit can continue with an analysis of other factors that may be relevant in a given situation. (Note the items listed under "Reasons . . ." at the bottom of Exhibit 5.3.[4])

---

[4]The question may have occurred to you, "Is it possible to have credibility that is *too high?*"Yes, if we take into account that people all too often place blind faith in anything that certain persons tell them. If, however, the communicator is possessed of integrity and wisdom, he or she will discourage listeners from becoming mindless devotees. Charisma has its place in modern life, but in very small doses and very special circumstances. Hitler and the Reverend Jones taught us how dangerous unrestrained charisma—which is the ultimate degree of credibility—can be. Modern managers need thinking human beings around them, not sheep.

An earlier part of this section stated that earning credibility can be a time-consuming project. The chapter will end with a caution: Never forget what I choose to call the Perverse Law of Credibility—the credibility that may have taken years to establish can be destroyed in a few seconds. Logically, this is grossly unfair. But that's the way it is.

References

Applbaum, Ronald L., and Karl W. Anatol. "The Factor Structure of Source Credibility as a Function of the Speaking Situation." *Speech Monographs* 39 (1972): 216-22.

Applbaum, Ronald L., and Karl W. Anatol. "A Rejoinder." *Speech Monographs* 41 (1974): 295-98.

Cronkhite, Gary, and Jo Liska. "A Critique of Factor Analytic Approaches to the Study of Credibility." *Speech Monographs* 43 (1976): 91-107.

D'Aprix, Roger M. *The Believable Corporation.* New York: Amacom, 1977.

Davis, Stanley M. "Transforming Organizations: The Key to Strategy Is Context." *Organizational Dynamics* 10, no. 3 (Winter 1982): 64-80.

Delia, Jesse G. "A Constructivist Analysis of the Concept of Credibility." *Quarterly Journal of Speech* 62 (1976): 361-75.

Deutsch, Arnold R. *The Human Resources Revolution.* New York: McGraw-Hill, 1979.

Drucker, Peter F. *Management—Tasks, Responsibilities, Practices.* New York: Harper & Row, 1974.

Falcione, Raymond L. "The Factor Structure of Source Credibility Scales for Immediate Superiors in the Organizational Context." *Central States Speech Journal* 25 (1974): 63-66.

Foehrenbach, Julie, and Karn Rosenberg. "How Are We Doing?" *Journal of Communication Management,* no. 4 (1982): 3-11.

Galbraith, John Kenneth. *The New Industrial State.* Boston: Houghton Mifflin, 1967.

Giffin, Kim. "The Contribution of Studies of Source Credibility to a Theory of Interpersonal Trust in the Communication Process." *Psychological Bulletin* 68 (1967): 104-20.

Gildea, Joyce A. "45,000 Employees Judge Effectiveness of Internal Communication." *Journal of Organizational Communication,* no. 2 (1981): 3-11.

Glauser, Michael J. "Self-Worth and Verbal Dominance as Predictors of Communication Behavior and Outcomes of Decision Making." Ph. D. dissertation, Department of Communication, Purdue University, West Lafayette, Ind., 1981.

Goodman, Ronald, and Richard S. Ruch. "In the Image of the CEO." *Public Relations Journal* 37, no. 2 (February 1981): 14-19.

Hayes, Robert H., and William J. Abernathy. "Managing Our Way to Economic Decline." *Harvard Business Review* 58, no. 4 (July-August 1980): 67-77.

Kanter, Rosabeth Moss. "Power Failure in Management Circuits." *Harvard Business Review* 57, no. 4 (July-August 1979): 65-75.

Katz, Daniel, and Robert L. Kahn. *The Social Psychology of Organizations,* 2nd ed. New York: Wiley, 1978.

Levinson, Harry. *The Great Jackass Fallacy.* Boston: Graduate School of Business Administration, Harvard University, 1973.

Littlejohn, Stephen W. "A Bibliography of Studies Related to Variables of Source Credibility." In *Bibliographic Annual in Speech Communication: Vol. II, 1971 Annual.* New York: Speech Communication Association, 1971, pp. 1-40.

Minter, Robert L. "A Comparative Analysis of Managerial Communication in Two Divisions of a Large Manufacturing Company." 4 vols. Ph. D. dissertation, Department of Communication, Purdue University, West Lafayette, Ind., 1969.

O'Boyle, Thomas F. "Steel's Management Has Itself to Blame." *Wall Street Journal,* May 17, 1983, p. 32.

Petzinger, Thomas, Jr. "Double Talk Grips Business Reports as Firms Try to Sugarcoat Bad News." *Wall Street Journal,* March 31, 1982, p. 25.

Redding, W. Charles. "The Organizational Communicator." In W. C. Redding and G. A. Sanborn, eds., *Business and Industrial Communication: A Source Book.* New York: Harper & Row, 1964, pp. 29-58.

Redding W. Charles. *Communication within the Organization.* New York and West Lafayette, Ind.: Industrial Communication Council and Purdue Research Foundation, 1972.

Richetto, Gary M. "Source Credibility and Personal Influence in Three Contexts: A Study of Dyadic Communication in a Complex Aero-space Organization." Ph. D. dissertation, Department of Communication, Purdue University, West Lafayette, Ind., 1969.

Simons, Herbert W., Nancy N. Berkowitz, and John R. Moyer. "Similarity, Credibility, and Attitude Change: A Review and a Theory." *Psychological Bulletin* 73 (1970): 1-16.

Stockdale, James Bond. "The World of Epictetus." In Peter J. Frost, Vance F. Mitchell, and Walter R. Nord, eds., *Organizational Reality: Reports from the Firing Line,* 2nd ed. Glenview, IL: Scott, Foresman, 1982, pp. 204-16.

Townsend, Robert. *Up the Organization.* New York: Knopf, 1970.

Whyte, William H., Jr. *Is Anybody Listening?* New York: Simon & Schuster, 1952.

CHAPTER 6

The Sensitive Communicator

The preceding chapter introduced you to the first four hallmarks of communication excellence. This chapter will be devoted exclusively to the fifth—*sensitivity*. In terms of the nine-step schedule (Chapter 2), we are still at Step 4: taking aim. We are still, in other words, concerned with identifying the basic characteristics of the ideal managerial communicator—and, by inference, of the ideal system of corporate communication. Indeed, the usefulness of a guidebook like this virtually ceases beyond Step 4, since all the remaining steps involve learning activities that only you can carry out—albeit with the assistance of other people.

INSENSITIVITY: THE MANAGER'S PUBLIC ENEMY NUMBER 1

"*Sensitivity training*" and "T-Groups" are phrases that were bandied about in business and social conversations throughout the 1960s and 1970s. In the mid-1980s we don't seem to hear so much about these activities; we are more likely to hear about assertiveness, "management by command," and gamesmanship. However, people's basic human needs for being treated with consideration and respect transcend all transitory fashions. And these needs are what sensitivity is really all about.

The best way to get a grip on sensitivity—admittedly a rather slippery concept—is to look around us and take note of what happens when it is present or absent. Reading philosophical essays on the subject is less likely to be helpful than close inspection of actual behavior. We begin by "accentuating the negative": that is, since insensitivity is so frequently brought forward as a charge against corporate management, it behooves us to see whether the charge is justified.

As clarification, we can note that, however we define it, sensitivity may be considered as (a) an attitude, (b) a form of knowledge or understanding, (c) an innate talent, (d) a learned behavioral skill, or any combination of these. In the present context, major emphasis will be upon (a) and (b): attitudes and understandings.

First, flip back the pages to the beginning of Chapter 5 and reread several of the quotations. The second finds much corporate communication to be "patronizing, condescending and simplistic." The third speaks of businesses treating people as "so many statistics." And the seventh suggests that management frequently treats employees as "jackasses." If we grant some truth to these accusations—and the evidence would hardly justify a flat denial—then we could say that they all describe familiar symptoms of a communication virus called insensitivity. The virus may infect the body of either an entire corporation (as an impersonal entity) or an individual manager (as a person).

The most familiar manifestations of insensitivity occur in instances where a communicator appears to be unaware that other people exist, or that they have feelings, aspirations, desires, needs, fears. In other words, the insensitive communicator is one who fails to adapt to the demands of the total communication situation, especially to his or her listeners or readers. Hence, we find ourselves applying such descriptors as the following:

Callous	Unfeeling
Condescending	Boring
Patronizing	Pompous
Insulting	Self-centered
Tactless	Unintelligible
Dictatorial	Living in an ivory tower

Examples of insensitivity in managerial communications include the following:

- As you may recall, in the 1970s National Airlines (now absorbed by another company) made a splash with an advertising campaign featuring pictures of attractive stewardesses, accompanied by slogans like "I'm Cheryl . . . Fly Me." Many women's groups attacked the ads as sexist. Finally, the company announced a new promotional slogan: "National Airlines—Take Me, I'm Yours." When questioned by a reporter who suggested that the new slogan was loaded with sexual connotations, a company spokesman was quoted as saying that he failed to see "any such connotations" (Cappo, 1976). We can observe, in passing, that this reply reflects the conveyor-belt fallacy (see Chapter 3).

- A large retailing firm tells its new employees on the first day of an intensive orientation course that they are "XYZ's people now," to be transformed into "absolute machines." The theme is hammered home: "Forget whatever you've learned in the past. From now on, you're going to do things our way." The inductees are also warned that elaborate electronic surveillance and accounting systems will mean that "we're always watching you, so don't think you can get away with goofing off or ignoring rules." The explicit use of the words "absolute machines" in the required orientation lecture suggests that, at least for this company, Deutsch was guilty of no exaggeration in accusing many employers of treating people like statistics to be "run through a computer" (1979, p. 28).
- A knowledgeable observer of corporate communication practices, Janine Ragan (managing editor of the *Ragan Report*), recently wrote a front-page editorial about "Tony Smith," a fifty-five-year-old worker on an assembly line who has been employed by the same company for thirty years. Here's an excerpt from the editorial (Ragan, 1983):

> Travelling home after work, Smith reads the local paper. He reads about the complex negotiations taking place in the Middle East; he reads that larger deficits cause higher interest rates; he reads technical articles . . . .
>
> The next morning, Smith goes to work, picks up the company paper and finds cartoons explaining his health benefit program, and crossword puzzles explaining company profits.
>
> It's as if Smith just can't comprehend any other way, as if he's 15 instead of 55. . . . Judging from some employee publications, anyone over the age of 25 is incoherent and unable to understand issues of complexity without the aid of puzzles.

Findings from several survey studies give us some idea of the extent of the problem. A few years ago, for the purpose of investigating causes of low job satisfaction and slumping productivity, the United States Maritime Commission sponsored a survey among managers and workers in eleven U.S. and Canadian shipyards. Among the major conclusions reported by the research director was this:

Many employees *believe* that management has no interest in them as persons, is unaware of what they do and is oriented to machines rather than to people. Company executives deny this.... Either they don't understand their own attitudes ... or they have not communicated them effectively to their employees. (Muench, 1978, p. 23; emphasis added.)

Probably the largest ongoing employee survey research in the United States, continued over a period of many years, is that conducted by the Opinion Research Corporation (ORC), of Princeton, New Jersey. Approximately 175,000 employees in about 160 client companies (ranging in size from fewer than 500 to more than 200,000 employees) have been surveyed in successive waves since 1975. A recent ORC report (Cooper et al., 1979) revealed that a "majority of hourly and clerical employees" gave unfavorable ratings to their companies on such matters as the following:

- "Respect shown to employees as individuals."
- "Willingness to listen to [employees'] problems and complaints."
- "Doing something about employees' problems and complaints."

We should note that managerial respondents, as well as employees, also registered varying degrees of dissatisfaction on these points—ranging between a third and a half of the sample. (A similar finding from a more recent ORC survey was reported at the beginning of Chapter 5, in the eighth quotation.)

The authors of the report expressed the opinion that insensitivity—failure to treat employees with respect as human beings—is a basic cause of substandard job performance, especially when "some of the major rewards for good performance are missing, and employees *perceive* that management makes many decisions arbitrarily" (Cooper et al., 1979, p. 124; emphasis added).

Similar results from other surveys could be cited; but we shall stop with one more example—Case 13. In this case we can read the exact words that employees directed to company management, providing us with a gut-level understanding of employees' reactions to what they perceived as managerial insensitivity.

CASE 13   Company I: Employees sound off

A few months after effecting a merger with a smaller firm, Company I conducted a wide-ranging survey to assess the effectiveness of management-employee communication. Management was dismayed to find high levels of employee dissatisfaction with several features of the total communication program, but especially with the manner in which the merger had been handled.

The survey included an invitation to the respondents to write whatever comments they wished, as supplements to the structured questionnaire items. Here are a few of the numerous comments that employees wrote: "We were officially informed [of the merger] *two days later* via a *press release.* Employees should have the right to know what's happening prior to public release." "Our people are the last to know about what's going on inside the Company." "There's an air of secrecy." " I've seen my attitude change from one of enthusiasm to one of apathy [because] of the lack of communication between management and hourly personnel. If an employee is made to feel that he is worth something—that his ideas are welcomed by management—the entire product of the Company will benefit."

Source: Survey report made available to the author.

Note that reactions like those cited above are employees' *perceptions.* Obviously, the managers of Company I were unaware of the fact that large numbers of employees perceived them as insensitive. Indeed, almost no managers are guilty of insensitivity because of stupidity or orneriness. No doubt the overwhelming majority of managers believe they are sensitive human beings. The problem is made even worse by the fact that most people are *unaware of their unawareness.* Hence, a basic goal of this chapter is to help you break through this vicious circle.

Recall now the quotation, listed seventh at the beginning of Chapter 5, from Harry Levinson, a respected psychologist and management consultant: "When people sense themselves to be viewed as jackasses, they will . . . resist hearing management's messages, no matter how clear the type or pretty the pictures" (1973, p. 11). Understandably, Levinson suggests that most management-employee communication may in fact be "a waste of time and money."

This gloomy view may easily be rhetorical hyperbole on Levinson's part. But convincing evidence can be found to support the conclusion that many managers are perceived by employees as treating them as if they were jackasses, children, or morons. Don't miss that key word *perceived.* A manager may, inside, be a deeply caring and sensitive person. But this fact becomes tragically irrelevant if others perceive him as unfeeling, callous, patronizing—that is, insensitive. Hence, the pivotal role of communication. If managers are perceived as insensitive, a close scrutiny of their messages—especially their unintentional messages—should lead to discovery of the factors causing such perceptions. (You may recall that a central objective of "sensitivity training" or "T-Group" experiences purports to be the improving of our ability to see ourselves as others see us.)

Sensitivity, then, reflects an all-encompassing cast of mind. It denotes a special kind of understanding, not only understanding other people, but above all understanding how other people perceive *us.* Let's pursue this a bit further.

TOWARD AN UNDERSTANDING OF UNDERSTANDING

Manager M, shall we say, "understands" that Employee E welcomes the chance to do overtime work at overtime pay. For years, M has "understood" that almost all employees value the additional income over a few extra leisure-time hours. However, let us suppose that E happens to be an individual who prefers the extra hours—in order to be with his family and to indulge his love of the weekend poker game. Let's suppose further that M and E very seldom talk with each other; M is rather aloof, and E is too reticent to "open up" with a boss. Thus, when E suddenly blows his top one Friday afternoon and in the heat of anger calls M an S.O.B. for notifying him to appear for overtime work the next morning, M is shocked. He regards E as an ingrate or a fool, or both. Once started, such a state of affairs can, of course, spiral into a destructively hostile relationship, perhaps eventuating in E's being fired. All the while, M never comprehends "what's bugging E."

What we are dealing with here happens to be the subject of much research and theorizing among social scientists (and clinicians) in recent years: how we form impressions—perceptions—of events or persons (Perception Level 1), how we perceive other people's perceptions of events (Perception Level 2), and how we perceive other people's perceptions of our own perceptions (Perception Level 3). As can easily be seen, when we try to explain the process in words, it gets complicated. Actually, however, in everyday life our brains are quite capable of making fantastic split-second calculations of all these—and even more—levels of perception. For example, Manager M perceived Employee E's perception of overtime work incorrectly. But he was not, of course, aware that this perception was incorrect. He was wrong without knowing that he was wrong!

To make our hypothetical situation worse, Employee E also arrived at an incorrect inference: that M was indifferent to his needs and desires. As a result, E perceived M as a manager who perceived himself (E) as a person motivated chiefly by money. In this belief (perception of M's perception), E was actually correct. But E was incorrect in believing that M cared nothing about his welfare. We know that M actually regarded himself as caring deeply about E's welfare and thought he was doing E a favor by providing overtime.

Then, taking it a step further (we court dizziness now!), we can also say that E's perception of M's-feeling-that-E-regarded-him-as-a-callous-manager was likewise correct. After E's blowup, M did indeed "understand" that E looked upon him as callous—which E did. We see, then, that a meeting of minds—where the two parties share only *some*, but not all, perceptions correctly—can be insufficient for achieving reciprocal understanding. (If you feel so inclined, you can carry this spiral of perceptions between M and E through several more levels. But you're on your own!)

Complicated as it no doubt appears, this progression of perceptions and perceptions-of-perceptions is actually occurring (in our heads, automatically) every time we communicate with others. In fact, if such a process did not take place, we would find it impossible to carry on meaningful communication for more than a few minutes. What we must remember is this: *Open, two-way communication, particularly reciprocal feedback, is the key to preventing or reversing spirals of mutual misunderstanding.* Put it this way: Any misunderstanding can cause trouble; but the trouble gets much worse when we remain ignorant of the fact that there *is* misunderstanding. Recall that Manager M and Employee E did not talk to each other very much; when they did, they said very little about their true feelings regarding the job, and even less about their feelings toward each other. The spiral of misunderstanding could have been prevented, or at least arrested early in the game, had E opened up and told M how he felt about working overtime. Also, M could have been a better communicator by encouraging E to open up—especially by the use of empathic listening.

For another example, recall Case 8 in Chapter 1 (Company F: The President and the Personnel Manager). Only after the intervention of a third-party consultant were these two individuals, despite having been close friends for years, able to exchange *some* two-way feedback—perceptions of each other's perceptions—thus clearing up *some* of the misunderstanding. Even then, however, they found it impossible to solve all their difficulties.[1]

Again, never forget that feedback—continuous and reciprocal—is the indispensable requirement for combatting misunderstanding. The feedback may be informal, like that occurring during a friendly social conversation; or it may be formal, like that obtained in corporate "speak-up" programs, morale surveys, suggestion systems, and the like.

DIMENSIONS OF MANAGERIAL SENSITIVITY

Concern for Others

To this point, we have been stressing the most obvious dimension of communicator sensitivity; namely, the degree to which the communicator (especially as a message sender) understands the person with

---

[1] This topic—perceptions and perceptions of perceptions—deserves much more attention than space permits here. What we are discussing comes under the rubric of "metaperception," a major issue in the recent theoretical literature. You are strongly urged to read an article by Kets de Vries (1979), which appeared in the *Harvard Business Review* under the alluring title "Managers Can Drive Their Subordinates Mad." If you have time to delve into the basic literature, I recommend going to two sources that are both readable and sophisticated: Laing, Phillipson, and Lee (1966 and 1972), and Watzlawick *et al.* (1967, pp. 90–93).

whom he or she is interacting. We could call this dimension *concern for others*. It is the dimension most commonly in the minds of critics like those cited earlier in the chapter—the ones who deplore "managerial insensitivity." The examples, you will recall, always illustrated the alleged failure of management to show concern for others (especially rank-and-file employees).

Clearly, this dimension is of immense importance. It is the basis of what we sometimes call *audience analysis*. However, as the preceding section shows, the really profound insights to be gained from audience analysis go beyond the customary demographics—like race, sex, age, or union affiliation—to explore successive levels of perceptions. What this means is that it's essential not only for managers to know the background of their subordinates, but especially to know how they perceive their jobs, how they perceive themselves, how they perceive the company, and (most difficult of all) how they perceive their managers.

Besides concern for others, there are additional dimensions of sensitivity. Two are of prime significance: (a) sensitivity to oneself (self-knowledge) and (b) sensitivity to the demands of the total communication situation. The first will be designated *concern for self;* the second, *awareness of situation*.

Concern for Self

At several points in earlier pages we have had occasion to talk about the established fact that all of us are frequently unaware of our own attitudes, assumptions, and needs. (No endorsement of the Freudian doctrine of the unconscious is intended here.) I acknowledge the epistemological problem of "knowing" what another person really feels (or believes, or needs). In fact, there is no way any of us can ever be certain about the feelings of another person. All we can do is make inferences, based upon our observations of behavior. However, such inferences must be taken seriously; and we can frequently use other people's inferences to enhance our self-knowledge.

Arterburn and Di Salvo recently reported their observations of a municipal personnel department (1982). About two years before their entry into the department as consultants, a new director had been appointed. Intensive interviews, conducted over a long period of time, revealed that the new manager was firmly convinced that he was engaging in Theory Y behavior. However, his fourteen subordinates were equally convinced that he was the epitome of Theory X management. (In fact, nine of fourteen staff members resigned following the arrival of the new director.) Whom are we to believe? The director, or fourteen close observers? I prefer to believe the observers. There is no suggestion here that the director was lying to the consultants; almost surely, he was telling them what he truly believed about himself.

Since the early 1970s, Chris Argyris, an eminent organizational theorist and practicing consultant, has been experimenting with what he calls *double-loop learning*. Working with experienced managers enrolled in seminars and training courses, Argyris and his associates have built their entire approach around role-playing exercises ingeniously designed to induce accurate self-awareness. According to Argyris, all of us acquire two sets of value premises—called *theories*—which serve as guidelines for dealing with other people. One set we are aware of. This set consists of those premises we openly acknowledge and frequently proclaim. The other set we are typically unaware of. Both sets influence our behavior, but the second is usually more powerful and more difficult to change, since it lies mostly beneath our level of consciousness. The names Argyris has coined to designate these two sets are, respectively, *espoused theories* and *theories in action* (Argyris, 1976; 1982a; 1982b).

For example, many managers (in common with many nonmanagers) espouse theories of open communication, disclosure of true feelings, and sharing of power. However, in the Argyris seminars, the managers' actual behavior usually contradicted these premises. When they found themselves embroiled in a difficult role play requiring discussion of a subordinate's shortcomings in job performance, these managers typically behaved in a manner designed "to win and not lose, to be in unilateral control, to suppress negative feelings" (Argyris, 1982a, p. 14; 1982b, pp. 21–22). To compound the problem, organizational members— even when they recognize contradictions between espoused theories and actions—find it threatening to acknowledge this fact. The result is what Argyris calls *undiscussability* (1982b, pp. 8–15).

This he illustrates by reproducing the probable mental processes occurring in the heads of a president and his subordinates:

> I (the president) know that I am playing games; you . . . know that I am playing games.
>
> You . . . are playing games; I (the president) know that you are playing games.
>
> All of us know that we should keep . . . the gameplaying undiscussable. (Argyris, 1982b, p. 8).

Thus, we see not only how important it is for us to know ourselves, especially by identifying our action premises, but also how very difficult this may be. In fact, without the aid of other people—from whom we can obtain feedback—complete self-awareness is impossible. As Argyris observes, although we are usually blind to our own action premises, other people can see our blindness—just as we can see other people's blindness. Hence, "other people will be crucial to our own learning" (1982b, p. 162).

Awareness of Situation

Awareness of situation refers to one's ability to understand the rules (usually informal and unstated) governing what is appropriate and what is inappropriate in a given communication episode. The person who tells locker-room jokes at a funeral is insensitive to the demands of the situation. Situational rules are particularly important in an organization, since by definition an organization is constituted by rules and norms defining what is expected of members occupying stated positions, in stated settings.

In his insightful book on the vagaries of human communication, *Crazy Talk, Stupid Talk,* Neil Postman places the highest priority on the communication situation—which he calls the *semantic environment*. He tells us that "What makes crazy talk crazy or stupid talk stupid is not the language people use but *the relationship of their remarks to the totality of the situation they are in*" (Postman, 1976, p. 10). Examples of communication situations requiring dramatically different communication behaviors, Postman points out, are the witness box, the confessional box, and the batter's box: "the batter, for example, who turns to the umpire and says, 'Father, I have sinned...' is either trying to make a bad joke or needs a psychiatrist instead of a priest or an umpire" (pp. 10–11).

All managers would do well to study carefully the invisible rules—and the conditions under which they can be bent or broken—governing such situations as:

Who should say what at a staff meeting.
Who can go over the boss's head, and how, and when.
What should be said face-to-face rather than by telephone.
What can and cannot be said to a subordinate at the annual picnic.
Approaching the manager of another department to broach the idea of joining forces on a budget proposal.
Obtaining inside information from unofficial sources (such as secretaries or staff specialists).
Participating in a brainstorming session.
Discussing a sensitive issue off the record with a union officer.

None of this is to imply that informal rules hold imperial sway over a manager's communication. All it says is that the totality of the situation must be taken into account. We are told that rules are made to be broken, and indeed they may be. But it is one thing to stumble into a violation of the rules, and quite another to defy them as an act of careful deliberation. Moreover, as Peters (1978) has shown, managers who make wise use of the powers inhering in their office can find ways to gracefully modify the rules, or create totally new ones. Even in these cases, however, the managers are highly sensitive to the demands and constraints entailed in each communication situation.

When we speak of the communication situation and of the unwritten rules surrounding it, we are dealing with facets of the corporate culture. The bedrock of any culture consists of rituals (don't call them "empty rituals"!), the accepted modes of behavior that authenticate the group or organization. In their discussion of work rituals and management rituals, Deal and Kennedy observe that "the most important management ritual continues to be the formal meeting" (1982, p. 70).

The same authors, in a different context, mention an example of an executive who deliberately broke with tradition but in doing so revealed his astute awareness of all factors in the situation. They report that Jack Welch (now CEO of General Electric), when he was a group executive, "had a special telephone installed in his office with a private number . . . made available to all the purchasing agents in his group." An agent getting a price concession from a vendor could thereby call Welch directly. "Whether he was making a million-dollar deal or chatting with his secretary, Welch would interrupt what he was doing, take the call and say: 'That's wonderful news . . .'" (Deal and Kennedy, 1982, p. 41).

THE KEY ATTRIBUTES OF THE SENSITIVE COMMUNICATOR

Let's pull all these ideas together to see whether we can delineate the most salient features of an ideal: the perfectly sensitive communicator. I propose a set of adjectives that can be arranged in a tabular form corresponding to the three facets of sensitivity: concern for others, concern for self, and awareness of the situation. The list can easily be used as a self-assessment rating chart, whereby a manager—at the end of the working day, for example—can check up on himself or herself.

What does it mean to be a sensitive communicator?

The SENSITIVE communicator is:
1. SUPPORTIVE, which means being especially: ⎤
   a. RECEPTIVE and   ⎬ CONCERN FOR OTHERS
   b. RESPONSIVE   ⎦

2. EXPRESSIVE   ⎤
3. ASSERTIVE   ⎬ CONCERN FOR SELF
                ⎦

4. PERCEPTIVE   ⎤ AWARENESS OF SITUATION
                ⎦

Before we look more closely at these attributes, we should remember that sensitivity can be applied to both the personal and corporate domains of managerial communication (see Chapter 4). However, in the present context we are starting at the personal level, focusing upon the way in which an individual manager is perceived as being more or less sensitive. The last chapter will address itself more directly to sensitivity at the over-all corporate level.

Supportive

The concept of "supportive supervision" has been promulgated by Likert and his associates at the University of Michigan as a fundamental component of their famous System 4 style of management (Likert, 1967, pp. 47-49). Supportive managers, according to Likert, are ones who engage in such behavior as the following:

They demonstrate trust in their subordinates.
They are helpful and empathic.
They show that they respect the individuality and integrity of subordinates; they give credit and recognition for good work.
They keep their subordinates informed.
They solicit ideas from their subordinates.

One of the most influential contributions to our understanding of supportiveness as an essential characteristic of good communication is the work of Jack Gibb, first published more than twenty years ago (Gibb, 1961). Basing his conclusions upon an analysis of hundreds of communication acts in small-group settings, Gibb postulated a set of six criteria of supportiveness, each matched by a polar opposite constituting "defensiveness." He defined defensive behavior as that "which occurs when an individual perceives threat or anticipates threat" (p. 141). By *threat* he meant primarily threat against one's sense of self-regard—one's self-respect or ego—rather than threat against material well-being.

Gibb's model of defensive versus supportive communication has been reprinted innumerable times, and several researchers have demonstrated the general validity of his basic concepts. Space limitations do not permit a discussion of the extensive literature generated by Gibb's work, but it is possible to summarize his core ideas.

Fundamentally, the supportive communicator is one who makes every effort to reduce perceived threat to the lowest possible level. More specifically, Gibb's work suggests to me that supportive managers are those who, in their communication:

- Avoid the impression of evaluating or criticizing the other person *as a person* (focusing instead upon nonevaluative description of observable, verifiable events).
- Avoid the impression of dominating, of exercising coercive control (focusing instead upon creating a spirit of collaboration between equals).
- Avoid the impression of pulling wires behind the scenes, of being sly manipulators (focusing instead upon candor and openness—willingness to talk about "hidden agenda").
- Avoid the impression of being cold, impersonal, calculating (focusing instead upon understanding how other people feel—on showing an attitude of concern, empathy).
- Avoid the impression of regarding themselves as some sort of superior beings (focusing instead upon self-confidence combined with respect for the integrity and worth of others).
- Avoid the impression of knowing all the answers, of being rigid dogmatists (focusing instead upon showing awareness of human fallibility, willingness to listen to new information—but at the same time forthrightness in stating and defending their convictions).

Receptive and Responsive

As used in the present context, the term *receptive* refers primarily to willingness to receive incoming feedback from others; the term *responsive*, primarily to willingness to give feedback to others. Hence, I propose the terms *feedback receptiveness* and *feedback responsiveness.*

Both of these qualities are essential if a manager is to combat that universal plague: managerial isolation. Given the unavoidable fact that, in almost any large organization, subordinates far outnumber managers, a certain degree of isolation is inevitable. Indeed, were any manager to attempt the staggering task of receiving and assimilating all the incoming information that all subordinates might wish to send, that manager would quickly die a symbolic death of information overload. (The basic function of organizational structure is actually to *restrict* the flow of messages in such a manner that the organization can get its work done without drowning in an ocean of information.)

However, the manager—while compelled to be selective—must find ways of obtaining the important information, especially feedback regarding his or her own job performance. Likewise, although unable to respond to every incoming message, the manager must find ways of being responsive—on a regular, continuing basis—to suggestions, inquiries, complaints, reports, and so on. Receptive and responsive managers are those, for example, who can:

- Cultivate good relationships (both formal and informal) with persons who are usually well informed about important happenings.
- Find trustworthy assistants who will filter out the low-priority from the high-priority incoming messages, and who (because of the manager's support) will fearlessly transmit—without watering down—the negative inputs.
- Selectively bypass formal lines on the organization charts and communicate directly (face to face whenever possible) with relevant persons in the company, regardless of rank or position.
- Create an atmosphere in which it is made unmistakably clear that people are rewarded, not penalized, for speaking out or for being the bearers of bad news.
- Act on the knowledge that time taken to respond candidly, promptly, and directly to significant questions or complaints from rank-and-file employees is not time stolen from the important business of managing—rather, it is of the very essence of effective managing.

An example of receptiveness and responsiveness was recently provided by Roger Smith, chairman of General Motors, who received a letter from an assembly-line worker challenging him to match—from his hoard of "tons and tons of money"—a $640 donation to the GM-UAW Care and Share food distribution program. The worker mentioned in his letter that Smith was widely regarded as unapproachable. Smith's response? First, a person-to-person telephone call to the letter writer, followed in the next mail by a personal check.[2]

You will no doubt detect a central theme running through most of what has been said on the topics of supportiveness, receptiveness, and responsiveness. That theme is, in one word, *reciprocity*—which means two-way communication, two-way feedback, two-way influence. No one has expressed this more neatly, as it applies to managerial behavior, than a well-known student of management, Mason Haire: "The amount of influence a superior has with his subordinates depends on the degree to which *they* can influence *him*" (Haire, 1964, p. 202; emphasis added).

Expressive and Assertive

Many people make the plausible, but unwarranted, inference that the sensitive manager is simply a "nice guy," if not a "namby-pamby." It's easy to jump to such a conclusion. Indeed—if nothing else enters into the picture—reciprocity of influence can slip into an indecisive, vacillating posture.

---

[2] AP dispatch, *Lafayette* (Ind.) *Journal and Courier*, Jan. 16, 1983, p. A-2.

But, as we have seen, concern for others is only one of three facets to sensitivity. The second, and equally important, facet is concern for self. And, so far as communication behavior is involved, this means the ability to express one's ideas and especially one's feelings, the ability to be articulate about one's own needs and values. It also means the ability to take risks, to state forthrightly one's convictions—in other words, to be assertive. Assertiveness training workshops, typically designed for women (whom our culture has tended to force into submissive roles), go to great pains to make this distinction: assertive is at an optimum midpoint between two equally dysfunctional extremes: servility and arrogance, or submission and dominance.

The person who is weak on concern for self is likely to display such characteristics as the following:

Retreating into silence or acquiescence at the first signs of opposition or displeasure (especially on the part of higher-power figures).
Engaging in various forms of ingratiation, such as flattery or sycophancy.
Sweeping potentially threatening issues under the rug.
Watering down or otherwise distorting reports thought to be disturbing to others (especially powerful others).
Maintaining a generally apologetic, servile demeanor.
Parroting or hitch-hiking on the ideas of others.

The person who is inordinately concerned with self (who may, in fact, be compensating for deep feelings of inadequacy) is easily recognized by display of behaviors diametrically opposite to those listed above. (The executive described in Case 7, Chapter 1, may have been such an individual: the company editor testified that the prime objective was always to make him look good.)

Perceptive

Perceptive is the adjective chosen to epitomize all the various ways in which a communicator may be aware or unaware of situational forces impinging upon a given communication episode. There is little need to add to what has been said earlier in the chapter regarding this topic.

What can a person do, then, to improve his or her ability to perceive the priorities in communication situations? Really, I suggest, only two things: (1) raise one's level of awareness by reading and discussion, so that one learns what to look for; and (2) throw oneself into "gutsy" role plays of realistic managerial episodes, always accompanied by candid feedback from observers (supplemented, when feasible, by feedback supplied by audio and video tapes).

The process of consciousness-raising with regard to all aspects of communication sensitivity may be enhanced by memorizing—yes, memorizing!—a simple graphic representation, shown in Exhibit 6.1. I call it the *sensitivity triad*. Communication sensitivity can be pictured as analogous to a tripod. All three legs are required if the structure is to survive. Similarly, a human being must combine three kinds of awareness—of self, of others, of situation—if communication is to be successful. No two of these are enough.

It may be helpful to think of two sets of combinations: Concern for self interacting with concern for others, and concern for self interacting with awareness of the communication situation. Although the possible combinations would approach the infinite, we can identify four anchor positions under each of these headings:

Concern for Self, Interacting with Concern for Others

1. *Low on self/high on others:* Typical descriptive terms: doormat, sycophant, echo chamber.
2. *Low on self/low on others:* calculating machine, ice cube.
3. *High on self/low on others:* bulldozer, egomaniac, manipulator, autocrat.
4. *High on self/high on others (the ideal):* sensitive, supportive, assertive, expressive.

Concern for Self, Interacting with Awareness of Situation

1. *Low on self/high on situation:* Typical descriptive terms: chameleon, weathervane, sacrificial lamb.
2. *Low on self/low on situation:* stumble-bum, clod.

EXHIBIT 6.1 The Sensitivity Triad

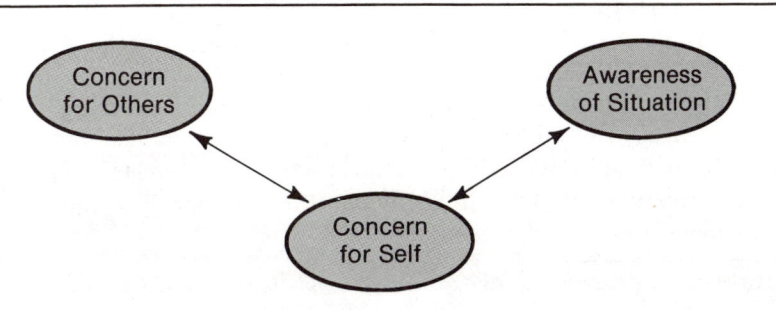

3. *High on self/low on situation:* loose cannon on a rolling deck.
4. *High on self/high on situation (the ideal):* sensitive, perceptive, assertive, expressive.

Questionnaires are another aid to self-assessment and self-improvement. Although any paper-and-pencil, self-report questionnaire is beset by multiple difficulties, both conceptual and metrical, such an instrument can be valuable in forcing the respondent to grapple with decisional choices. It happens that there exists a questionnaire specifically designed to measure communication sensitivity. This is the RHETSEN (rhetorical sensitivity) scale devised by Hart and Burks (1972) and refined by a number of researchers during the past decade.

The essense of rhetorical sensitivity, according to Hart and his associates, is *adaptation:* adaptation to the feelings of other persons and to the requirements of particular situations. This adaptation applies most directly to the communicator as a message sender (although listening is not ignored) and to his or her decisions about what may appropriately be said, when it may be said, to whom it may be said—and when it is appropriate to keep silent. Admittedly, therefore, the RHETSEN scale does not encompass the entire scope of sensitivity as presented here. But it does probe many attitudes significantly related to sensitive communication behavior.

The rhetorically sensitive person is described as one who occupies a moderate position between two polar extremes: being obsessed with self versus becoming a different self in every situation (Hart, Carlson, and Eadie, 1980, pp. 2-5). The person at the former extreme—excessive concern for self—has been labeled "The Noble Self"; the person at the other extreme—abnegation of self—"The Rhetorical Reflector." Thumbnail sketches of these hypothetical types describe Noble Selves as people who "see any variation from their personal norms as hypocritical, as a denial of integrity, as a cardinal sin" and Rhetorical Reflectors as people who "have no Self to call their own. For each person and for each situation they present a new self" (Darnell and Brockriede, 1976, p. 176; quoted in Hart, Carlson, and Eadie, 1980, p. 3).[3]

It can be seen that in making so few distinctions, the RHETSEN scale remains a relatively blunt instrument (as its authors concede). Nonetheless I recommend that you administer the RHETSEN scale to yourself. An abbreviated version, consisting of the twelve items found to discriminate best between high and low scorers, appears in Exhibit 6.2.

Your answers to the RHETSEN items are not nearly so important in

---

[3]Two Ph. D. dissertations, both completed at Purdue University, have investigated the applicability of the rhetorical sensitivity scale to organizational contexts; the second one found significant differences in communication behavior—in a simulated boss-subordinate setting—between persons with high Noble-Self scores and those with high Rhetorical sensitivity scores. See Carlson, 1978, and McCallister, 1981.

The Key Attributes of the Sensitive Communicator 99

EXHIBIT 6.2 RHETSEN Scale—Short Version[a]

Indicate the extent of your agreement or disagreement with each statement by writing in one of the following symbols:

A = Almost always true   D = Infrequently true
B = Frequently true   E = Almost never true
C = Sometimes true

1. _____ It's better to speak your gut feelings than to beat around the bush.
2. _____ A person should tell it like it is.
3. _____ When someone has an irritating habit, he or she should be told about it.
4. _____ A person who speaks his or her gut feelings is to be admired.
5. _____ You should tell someone if you think they are giving you bad advice.
6. _____ Saying what you think is a sign of friendship.
7. _____ It's best to hide one's true feelings in order to avoid hurting others.
8. _____ When someone dominates the conversation, it's important to interrupt them in order to state your opinion.
9. _____ One should keep quiet rather than say something which will alienate others.
10. _____ If you're sure you're right, you should argue with a person who disagrees with you.
11. _____ If people would open up to each other the world would be better off.
12. _____ You should tell people if you think they are about to embarrass themselves.

[a] Items selected and arranged by W. C. Redding. Author of the scale is Dr. Roderick P. Hart, professor of speech communication, University of Texas, Austin. For the complete forty-item scale, see Hart, Carlson, and Eadie (1980, pp. 6-7). I do not recommend that you attempt to derive a precise numerical score. The more times you answered *C*, the more likely it is (supposedly) that you are a rhetorically sensitive person. The more times you answered either *A* or *E*, the more likely it is that you *might* be either a "Noble Self" or a "Rhetorical Reflector"—depending upon the nature of the item.

themselves as the reasoning you went through to arrive at them. No doubt you found yourself frequently thinking, "Well, it all depends..." But then, that is the whole point of the exercise.

A note of caution: Sensitivity should never be equated with avoiding harsh reality or suppressing controversy merely for the sake of "being nice." As Argyris (1982b, p. 62) has demonstrated in his managerial role-playing experiments, camouflaging or "easing-in" approaches to handling unpalatable facts (regarding a subordinate manager's deficiencies in job performance) were no more effective than callous brutality.

Keep in mind that even a no-holds-barred argument acknowledges the fact that one's antagonist is worthy of notice. As Watzlawick, Beavin, and Jackson (1967, p. 86) point out, telling a person "You are wrong" is drastically different from ignoring that person—which is tantamount to saying "You don't exist." Jablin conducted an ingenious field experiment in which he exposed 385 persons, all subordinates in business firms, to different versions of a videotape simulating a situation in which a subordinate related bad news to his manager. An unequivocal finding was that the subjects found a "disconfirming" response by the manager—a

EXHIBIT 6.3 *Examples of Sensitive and Insensitive Managerial Communication with Subordinates*

Sensitive communicators will generally do these things **more** often	Sensitive communicators will generally do these things **less** often
Use a counseling approach: "How can I help?"	Make clear who's the boss: "Just *do* it!"
"Let's face it: This is the third time the coffee grounds got into the word processor."	"Three times and you're out! Tell me: How do you manage to be so careless?"
"Well, frankly, I have a hard time accepting that idea. Can you tell me more?"	"Only a damned fool would say a think like that!"
"You know, I've about come to the conclusion that I miscalculated the costs on this. How do *you* feel?"	"Sure, I'm running over budget. What do you expect from those ninnies in that ivory tower up on the forty-ninth floor!"
"I realize this may go against what you've been doing up to now. But let's lay out the pros and cons."	"Now look—we all have to take our lumps. If just trust my judgment and hang in there, you'll come out fine."
"I'd like us both to put down *in writing* the problems that you have faced in trying to meet these goals we agreed upon last year. Then we'll compare notes. Be sure to include any places where *I've* not given you the support you expected."	"It's my job to come up with a rating of your performance—which, as we both know, has fallen somewhat short of the objectives you yourself agreed to a year ago. Now here's how *I* diagnose the situation."
"That report had exactly the kind of statistical analyses we needed; not only that, it was readable! Remind me to pick up the next tab at Georgino's—and the sky's the limit!"	Keep silent.
"Well, frankly, I do feel that my record has been pretty damned good on this; so naturally it'll take some hard evidence to convince me I should change course. However, I wouldn't want it said of me two years from now that I was a stubborn old mule, either!"	"All you gotta do is look at my record! Can anyone around here match it? Come on. I'm asking you to come up with a name, if you can think of one. Of course you can't! Nothing succeeds like success, right? If there's nothing wrong, don't fix it!"
"Wow! This could be rough on both of us, couldn't it? I know you're in the exposed position—but don't forget that I'm still responsible. The buck stops here."	"I hate to tell you this, Janet, but you're simply going to have to take most of the heat on this. After all, I've been in this position for ten years, and a lot of people depend on me to shield them from all the crap that headquarters dumps onto *my* shoulders. It's your turn now."

EXHIBIT 6.3 *Examples of Sensitive and Insensitive Managerial Communication Continued*

"It's the sort of thing we can't ignore, Bill. As it looks to me, there has been a serious violation of section 6-B of the ethical practices code. I've always had faith in your judgment, and I'm listening with an open mind."	Avoid seeing Bill at all; instead do two things: 1. Send Bill a formal memo: "Pursuant to procedures stipulated in EPC, Sec. 6-B, you are hereby instructed to transmit to me, within 48 hours of noon today, the following documents: . . ." 2. Talk to the boss, at lunch, in a restaurant: "Well, our whiz kid finally went too far this time!"

response that ignored the subordinate—far less acceptable than a "disagreeing" one (Jablin, 1978, pp. 304–305).

To conclude this discussion you will find a table, in Exhibit 6.3, showing just a few of the communicative acts that we might expect the truly sensitive manager to display most of the time. These are paired in each case with a contrasting example representing what we should expect the sensitive manager to avoid most of the time. As you can see, the list does no more than scratch the surface. You can add many more examples of your own.

THE HUMAN DIGNITY AXIOM

An epitome of everything discussed in this chapter under the heading of the fifth hallmark of excellence—sensitivity—is articulated as the human dignity axiom:

> A manager's communication must demonstrate that other people (especially those holding subordinate positions) are regarded as mature adults, to be accorded the respect due all human beings. (This axiom presupposes that managers also maintain their own self-respect.)

A significant number of U.S. companies are making serious efforts to build their entire management practice upon this axiom. One of the more famous is Hewlett-Packard, with headquarters in Palo Alto, California (the highly publicized Silicon Valley area). A formal company document, *The HP Way* (1977), expounds "the belief that men and women want to do a good job, a creative job, and that if they are provided the proper environment they will do so." Hence, each individual is to be treated "with consideration and respect" in accord with the basic premise of "the dignity and worth of the individual" (pp. 2–3).

What happens to the human dignity axiom in the harsh light of corporate reality? We explore this question in the next chapter.

References

Argyris, Chris. "Leadership, Learning, and Changing the Status Quo." *Organizational Dynamics* 4, no. 3 (Winter 1976): 29-43.

Argyris, Chris. "The Executive Mind and Double-Loop Learning." *Organizational Dynamics* 11, no. 2 (Autumn 1982): 5-22. (a)

Argyris, Chris. *Reasoning, Learning, and Action: Individual and Organizational.* San Francisco: Jossey-Bass, 1982. (b)

Arterburn, David, and Vincent Di Salvo. "Theory X, Theory Y and Communication Style: Is There Really a Difference?" Paper presented at annual convention, American Business Communication Association, New Orleans, October 21, 1982.

Cappo, Joe. "Marketing." *Chicago Daily News,* July 30, 1976, business section.

Carlson, Robert E. "Rhetorical Sensitivity: Theoretical Perspective, Measurement, and Implications in an Interpersonal and Organizational Context." Ph. D. dissertation, Department of Communication, Purdue University, West Lafayette, Ind., 1978.

Cooper, M. R., B. S. Morgan, P. M. Foley, and L. B. Kaplan. "Changing Employee Values: Deepening Discontent?" *Harvard Business Review* 57, no. 1 (January-February 1979): 117-25.

Darnell, Donald, and Wayne Brockriede. *Persons Communicating.* Englewood Cliffs, NJ: Prentice-Hall, 1976.

Deal, Terrence E., and Allan A. Kennedy. *Corporate Cultures—the Rites and Rituals of Corporate Life.* Reading, MA: Addison-Wesley, 1982.

Deutsch, Arnold R. *The Human Resources Revolution.* New York: McGraw-Hill, 1979.

Gibb, Jack R. "Defensive Communication." *Journal of Communication* 11 (1961): 141-48.

Haire, Mason. *Psychology in Management,* 2nd ed. New York: McGraw-Hill, 1964.

Hart, Roderick P., and Don M. Burks. "Rhetorical Sensitivity and Social Interaction." *Speech Monographs* 39 (1972): 75-91.

Hart, Roderick P., Robert E. Carlson, and William F. Eadie. "Attitudes Toward Communication and the Assessment of Rhetorical Sensitivity." *Communication Monographs* 47 (1980): 1-22.

Hewlett-Packard Company. *The HP Way.* Palo Alto, Calif.: Public Relations Department, Hewlett-Packard, 1977.

Jablin, Fredric M. "Message-Response and 'Openness' in Superior-Superior-Subordinate Communication." Ph. D. dissertation, Department of Communication, Purdue University, West Lafayette, Indiana, 1981.

Kets de Vries, Manfred F. R. "Managers Can Drive Their Subordinates Mad." *Harvard Business Review* 57, no. 4 (July-August 1979): 125-34.

Laing, R. D., H. Phillipson, and A. R. Lee. *Interpersonal Perception.* New York: Springer, 1966; Harper & Row, Perennial Library, 1972.

Levinson, Harry. *The Great Jackass Fallacy.* Boston: Graduate School of Business Administration, Harvard University, 1973.

Likert, Rensis. *The Human Organization: Its Management and Value.* New York: McGraw-Hill, 1967.

McCallister, Linda. "'Rhetorical Sensitivity,' Sex of Interactants, and Superior-Subordinate Communication." Ph. d. dissertation, Department of Communication, Purdue University, West Lafayette, Indiana, 1981.

Muench, George. "It's Time to Put in Practice What We Already Know About Communication." *Journal of Organizational Communication* no. 3 (1978): 22–23.

Peters, Thomas J. "Symbols, Patterns, and Settings: An Optimistic Case for Getting Things Done." *Organizational Dynamics* 7, no. 2 (Autumn 1978): 2–23.

Postman, Neil, *Crazy Talk, Stupid Talk.* New York: Delacorte, 1976.

Ragan, Janine. "As It Seems to Others: Don't Tell Them What They Already Know" (editorial). *Ragan Report,* May 2, 1983, p. 1.

Watzlawick, Paul, Janet H. Beavin, and Don D. Jackson. *Pragmatics of Human Communication.* New York: Norton, 1967.

CHAPTER 7

Idealism Confronts Reality: People, Power, and Politics

The preceding chapter was devoted to the fifth hallmark of excellence—sensitivity. The picture it painted of the completely sensitive manager was intentionally idealistic. But you may be wondering, "Wouldn't this sensitive manager be chewed up very quickly in the real corporate world?" Unquestionably, many sensitive managers have indeed been chewed up. What, then, is to be done?

There are those who, in despair, counsel managers to master the fine art of "fighting dirty." However, even if we brush aside the ethical problems, I submit that such instruction would lie beyond both the scope and the competence of this book! Without ignoring the harsh realities of many corporate environments, the present chapter begins with a consideration of the sixth and final hallmark of excellence—imagination.* It then focuses attention upon ways in which managers can apply imagination to the communication problems associated with the exercise of power, the existence of corporate politicking, and the intricacies of interpersonal relationships.

The chapter will argue that, by applying imagination, managers can arm themselves with legitimate, ethically defensible weapons, such as the tactics of honest negotiation and advocacy. Although the emphasis will shift from the ideal to the pragmatic, I will modify nothing previously said about the crucial role of managerial sensitivity.

As the term is used here, *imagination* is intended to embrace what we generally think of when we use such words as *innovativeness*, inge-

---

Note: Since this chapter went to press, the following article has appeared: Manuel Velasquez, Dennis J. Moberg, and Gerald F. Cavanagh; "Organizational Statesmanship and Dirty Politics." *Organizational Dynamics* 12, no. 2 (Autumn 1983):65–80.

nuity, creativity, nonconformism. It connotes especially the ability to juxtapose familiar entities in previously unheard-of combinations.

To illuminate what imagination can mean in the corporate-communication context, one brief example will serve: Deutsch (1979) relates how a manufacturer of mine safety equipment used an ingenious communication technique to combat a pervasive problem in modern industry—"the isolation of individual workers from the end products of their work" (with negative effects upon motivation). This company transported its entire work force, in a fleet of buses, to a coal mine 200 miles distant. "There company people talked to miners whose lives depended on the equipment they produced, and visited the mine to see it in use. The effect upon morale, pride of workmanship, and quality control is said to have been enormous" (p. 135).

You might want to look over the media, channels, audiences, modalities, and techniques listed in Chapter 4, pages 43–46, to get an idea of the almost infinite number of ways in which these variables can be combined to create imaginative communication possibilities.

LISTENING TO OUR METAPHORS

A highly recommended device for stirring up the creative juices is to play a kind of mental game with ourselves to see how many different metaphors we can generate for describing a selected phenomenon: a person, a group, a physical object, a job, a company. In recent years, writers representing a wide variety of specializations (ranging from philosophy to engineering) have produced a considerable literature dealing with the profound influences metaphors can exercise in our lives. One of the best ways, for instance, to identify a manager's style of managing is to listen carefully for the metaphors he or she uses when referring to the company, to the job, and to employees.

As a writer, discussing managerial communication in the *Harvard Business Review,* observed, "The imagery and metaphors that a person frequently uses can be clues to understanding the world he or she inhabits . . . what's valued, what's feared, and what the speaker's behavioral rules are . . . ." (McCaskey, 1979, p. 136). His advice to managers—like yourself—who are interested in improving their communication effectiveness is: "Think of your metaphors."[1]

Following McCaskey's suggestion, take a few moments to consider what metaphors come to mind when you think of *the company*. How

---

[1]You are urged to read the McCaskey article; then, if you desire to pursue the exciting possibilities of metaphor analysis, browse through the collection of essays in Ortony (1979) or study the little book by Lakoff and Johnson, *Metaphors We Live By* (1980).

many of the following metaphors could be accurate descriptions, either of the company as a whole or of certain aspects of it:

Big happy family	Cornucopia	Zoo
Athletic team	Santa Claus	Volcano
Military unit	Battlefield	Police department
Well-oiled machine	Disneyland	Insane asylum
Play pen	Circus	Garbage can
Penitentiary	Garden	Snake pit
Pyramid	Boiling cauldron	Steamroller
Circle	Dragon	Swamp

Is it unreasonable to predict that the manager who thinks of the company as a "snake pit" will behave and will manage in ways dramatically different from the manager who thinks of the company as a "garden" (where human potentialities are carefully nourished)? We are back to circular causality again: our experiences induce us to create certain metaphors to comprehend those experiences; but then the metaphors, once created, can become unseen governors pushing our actions in this or that direction.

The well-known organizational psychologist Karl Weick calls our attention, in this context, to the *self-fulfilling prophecy* (Weick, 1979, pp. 50-51). For example, he reminds us how often people in both academic and corporate circles use military metaphors when they talk about organizations. We commonly hear such terms as *chain of command, troops, flank attack, retreat, mutiny, discipline.* "If," Weick suggests, "I assume that doing business is like waging war, then this presumption creates the very wars that I predicted." Thus, as military metaphors become more entrenched [whoops!] in their minds, some managers come to prefer the safe over the risky while other managers prefer combat to persuasion, or espionage to openness. Another instance of the self-fulfilling prophecy is found in Levinson's warning (mentioned in earlier chapters) against the pernicious effects of the "jackass" metaphor.

MYTH VERSUS REALITY

In the last few years critics have charged that even the most sophisticated, research-based theories of management are grievously inconsistent with the realities of corporate life. They point to the pervasive, but subtle, influence of metaphors (like those with origins in the military and the Catholic Church) as fountainheads of many taken-for-granted notions about the way organizations are supposed to work. For example, the traditional bureaucracy—a structure that, with minor variations, dominates the great majority of contemporary organizations—is basically an enactment of the "machine" metaphor (see, for example, March & Simon, 1958, pp. 36-48).

According to the conventional view, the successful business organization is a rational entity, depending upon rational planning, rational coordination, and rational decisions, all mobilized to achieve rational goals. Organizational effectiveness, we are told, results when members suppress their individual differences and pool their energies in a concerted team effort to serve the common good. Consensus is said to be the best foundation upon which to build corporate success. Disorder and conflict are generally regarded as aberrations, undermining both good human relations and efficiency.

But to what degree is this conventional view more myth than reality? Some close observers have argued that it is largely a myth, and—like most myths—one that "dies hard" (Zaleznik & Kets de Vries, 1975, p. 20). Consensus, declares Warren Bennis (at one time president of the University of Cincinnati) is probably a "folk dream" (Bennis, 1974, p. 54). Robert H. Miles of the Harvard Business School concludes that *purely rational conditions seldom obtain*" in real-life business firms (Miles, 1980, p. 157).

Perhaps the most devastating attack upon the textbook picture of the organization comes from the sociologist Charles Perrow, one of the most respected authorities on organizational behavior. He began a recent lecture with the declaration that our current "theories of organizations are busily shoring up a picture of the world of organizations that never existed." The real organizational world, he continued, is one where "organizational insanity frequently rules," a world full of "scandals, frustrations, ineptitudes, corruption, inaction, negligence, and inhuman error" (Perrow, 1980, pp. 1, 2).

The point is that much of the theory currently being promulgated is based upon false premises, derived from inaccurate descriptions of what really goes on. These popular theories—many of them involving prescriptions about "human relations" and "good communication"—are built upon the assumption that if we would only apply "a certain set of procedures, techniques, philosophies, and so on, any organization which is not operating both rationally and cooperatively could be made to do so" (Frost, Mitchell, & Nord, 1982, p. xiii).

For example, an extensive literature, produced over a period of decades, is based upon the assumption that an organization "has" a set of goals or objectives, agreed upon by a working consensus of organizational members. And, going back at least as far as Chester Barnard's seminal lectures of 1937 (Barnard, 1938), we have been told that one of the manager's highest-priority communication responsibilities is to articulate and inculcate these overarching goals. Indeed, no one could quarrel with this recommendation as a desirable ideal. However, such a principle can be misleading unless carefully qualified by recognition that numerous subgoals, many of them conflicting, also exist in the organization. As Frost, Mitchell, and Nord point out, what we frequently find is that "members at all levels of the organization ... pursue their own interests at the expense of others in the organization as well as at the expense of the achievement of the goals of a total organization" (1982, p. xiv). (See communication responsibility number 1, discussed in Chapter 4, page 54.)[2]

So . . . what are we to conclude? Are we to renounce the first five hallmarks of excellence? Are we to resign ourselves to the doleful prediction that qualities like self-worth, integrity, wisdom, credibility, and sensitivity are fine for some never-never land, but that they simply won't work in the real world of business—a world that "conceals a good deal of the law of the jungle beneath its surface of cordial behavior" (Zaleznik & Kets de Vries, 1975, p. 250)? Not at all. But we do need to apply wisdom and imagination to the task of finding ways of dealing with the harsh realities, while at the same time being able to live with ourselves—maintaining our integrity. We shall single out for special attention the communication problems related to power and to politics (politics is the use of strategy to deal with power).

THE REALITY OF CORPORATE POLITICS

In-house politics seems all too often to be treated as the Victorians treated sex: everybody knows it exists, but nobody wants to talk about it in public. For example, a common experience of researchers when they enter an organization is to find that informants have no difficulty whatever in identifying who wields power (actual power, that is, not necessarily formal authority) and in describing a long list of political (power) tactics known to be used in the company. But only in the last few years have a few hardy souls actually discussed internal politics as an inherent feature of all sizable organizations. In the words of Virginia Schein, a business school professor: "Power struggles, alliance formation, strategic maneuvering and 'cut-throat' actions may be as endemic to organizational life as planning, organizing, directing and controlling" (1977, p. 64).

Are corporate politics basically any different from politics on the

---

[2]For a summary of the numerous attacks upon conventional organization theory, especially what frequently goes under the rubric of "good human relations and communication," see two highly readable books: *Complex Organizations: A Critical Essay* (Perrow, 1979); and *The Gold and the Garbage in Management Theories and Prescriptions* (Lee, 1980).

national scene? No, except for "the subtlety of the voting procedure" (Zaleznik & Kets de Vries, 1975, p. 111). Even religious organizations have their internal political machinations, sometimes played out in a no-holds-barred arena: see, for example, the absorbing account of Vatican politics in Father Andrew Greeley's 1979 best-seller *The Making of the Popes 1978*.

Why should politics—that is to say, power maneuvering—be "endemic to organizational life"? The inevitability of corporate politics is summarized below as a set of premises.

> *Premise 1.* Division of labor is at the heart of any organization. Without segmentation no organization could function.
>
> *Premise 2.* Departmentalization and job specialization combine to encourage the development of goals associated with the enhancement of the unit or of the job specialty, or both. These goals are not ordinarily the same as, and sometimes are not even consistent with, the goals of the organization as a whole.
>
> *Premise 3.* It takes power to achieve goals; hence, individuals and groups will naturally seek to acquire enough power to gain their ends.
>
> *Premise 4.* Typically, power is unequally distributed in an organization. Some individuals and some groups have more power than others. Those with less power attempt to gain more.
>
> *Premise 5.* Power derives from control over resources (both physical and symbolic). If resources are relatively limited—as they almost always are—then individuals or groups confront a situation in which there are not enough resources to satisfy every party's power needs.
>
> *Premise 6.* Hence, parties try to find ways of securing larger shares of the available resources. One of the most useful—and at the same time "civilized"—ways of doing this is political maneuvering. (A less acceptable way is brute force.)

If this line of reasoning is correct—and I believe it to be so—we can see why internal politicking is inherent in any organization large and diverse enough to harbor individuals or groups marching to different drummers. A social scientist who has devoted much of his career to the study of corporate politics provides us with a useful definition. "Organizational politics," writes Jeffrey Pfeffer, "involves those activities taken within organizations to acquire, develop, and use power and other resources to obtain one's preferred outcomes in a situation in which there is uncertainty or dissensus about choices" (Pfeffer, 1981, p. 7).

DEPENDENCY AND LIMITED RESOURCES

Power does not exist in a vacuum. Person A's power is meaningful only in relation to Person B's power. Moreover, seldom if ever would we encounter a situation in real life—even in military dictatorships or prisons—in which one party has all the power, and the others none. After all, subjects do rebel, and prisoners do stage hunger strikes and riots.

The truth of the matter is that if we must rely upon some other person or group to satisfy any of our needs, then that person or group automatically has power over us. "So long as we need the services of others," as Kipnis has observed, "we are never far from the world of power" (Kipnis, 1976, p. 1). In other words, *power is a function of dependency*. We recognize this fact when we recall how much real power (as distinguished from formal authority) persons in modest positions can exercise.

The irony is that, as Kotter has shown, the higher we ascend in the corporate hierarchy, the more dependent we become upon others—hence, higher-level officers may easily possess less power than some of those holding lower-level positions (Kotter, 1979, p. 61). An organization can be defined, in fact, as a network of dependencies. In the modern corporation, who can get along without the services of others? Certainly not the CEO at the pinnacle of the pyramid. As Kotter points out, every manager is "at the mercy of superiors, subordinates, peers in other parts of the organization, subordinates of peers, outside suppliers, customers, competitors, unions, regulating agencies—the list could go on and on" (1979, p. 10).

Note that dependency occurs primarily in the presence of limited resources. Were resources unlimited, no manager would be dependent upon anyone else. But resources are never unlimited, even when they are abundant. There's always some additional resource we need (or think we need). Thus, "conflict over allocation of scarce resources" means that "*organizations inevitably become competitive systems*" (Nord & Durand, 1978, pp. 16–17). And as soon as competition arises, so does the likelihood that people will be tempted to use any means available to protect their interests.

Competition for limited resources therefore encourages the formation of *alliances* or *coalitions*—combinations made up of already existing groups that join forces in the hope that by pooling their separate resources they will gain more clout. Thus, articles and books now on the market proclaim the "coalition model" as the best way to describe corporate life (see especially Pfeffer & Salancik, 1977; Bacharach & Lawler, 1980). The authors of such works propose the "bargaining" metaphor as the most useful prism for viewing what goes on in real-life organizations.

This point of view carries important implications for managerial communication. If we observe typical managers in typical corporations, what will we find them doing? According to Bacharach and Lawler, we will find them "perpetually bargaining, repeatedly forming and reforming coalitions, and constantly availing themselves of influence tactics" (1980, p. 1). If this is an accurate description of reality, Pfeffer and Salancik are right in concluding that the manager occupies a "role similar to that of a politician—an assimilator and processor of demands" (1977, p. 21).

If, then, managers are politicians (at least much of the time), how should they communicate? According to *Fortune* magazine, a manager's effectiveness depends upon a "delicate balance between the powers of persuasion and coercion" (quoted by Peters, 1978, p. 15). In a similar vein, Pfeffer makes a powerful case for drastically revising business school curricula to equip modern MBAs with skills of advocacy, presentation, and language, especially in a context emphasizing power and politics (1981, pp. 354-55).

The inevitable question must now be faced: Isn't it true that, by definition, political tactics—and the kinds of communication associated with them—require us to cut ethical corners?

No one has to be told that the very word *politics* has suffered from a bad press—this despite the fact that politics is the only method yet devised for making a democracy work. "If politics is the pursuit and exercise of power over other human beings," declared David Wise in his book *The Politics of Lying* (1973), "truth is always likely to take a secondary role to that primary objective" (p. 24). And Bacharach and Lawler, who have written an entire treatise devoted to the proposition that we must understand organizations as political entities, concede that "deception and manipulation are intrinsic aspects of the political game," a game in which the parties typically "fake, bluff, and lie" in order to gain advantage over their antagonists (Bacharach & Lawler, 1980, pp. 120-22). Note the term *intrinsic*. It makes the strong assertion that dishonest communication methods inevitably characterize political behavior. If dishonesty, then, is truly inevitable in political communication, we may as well toss aside not only this book but all books like it and all educational activities designed to inculcate better communication.

In fact, some workshops and training seminars being advertised these days seem to accept the premise that bargaining and negotiating—the core of political communication—can only succeed by use of questionable tactics. Here's an example: One brochure promotes a course for managers with the promise that enrollees will master such techniques as "delays, diversions, face-saving devices, play-acting, omission of points, threats, creating confusion, walking out, and non-ethical ploys." From this description one might suppose that the course focuses upon conventional management-union collective bargaining tactics. Such, however, is not the case. We are assured that these skills apply to most aspects of the typical manager's job!

One source of difficulty in understanding political communication, I am convinced, lies in that familiar area of hidden assumptions, which were talked about in Chapter 3. What do parties do when they engage in politicking? Much of what they do we would call bargaining. However, what are our assumptions about bargaining? How do we (implicitly) define *bargaining*?

Bacharach and Lawler, in their definitive theoretical book, define bargaining as the "*give-and-take* that occurs when two or more interdependent parties experience a *conflict of interest*" (1980, p. 108; emphasis added). Reflect upon the italicized phrases. *Give-and-take* obviously suggests that there must be some sort of reciprocity in all bargaining: Each party gives something, each party gets something. A one-way encounter is either submission to coercion or acquiescence to persuasion; it is not bargaining. But consider carefully the other italicized phrase, *conflict of interest*. Even a reading of the Bacharach and Lawler book leaves one uncertain whether they are using this term to refer to *incompatible* objectives and values or simply to *different* objectives and values. Since these authors speak repeatedly of "deception and manipulation" as "intrinsic" features of political bargaining, one may infer that *conflict of interest* denotes only incompatibility, and ignores mere difference.

We may have here another example of the self-fulfilling prophecy (and again, one nurtured by the metaphors in our heads). If we assume from the outset that *all* bargaining or negotiating takes place between parties with incompatible goals, then we automatically adopt a win-lose posture. One party must win, the other must lose. When we start from this premise, it is but a small step to the belief that both parties will try to win at all costs, and another small step to the conclusion that all bargaining—and hence all political maneuvering in the corporation—must be dirty. There would be no room for clean politics.

That dirty tactics abound no one can deny. (For comprehensive inventories of shady political moves, see Miles, 1980, chap. 6; and Kipnis, Schmidt, & Wilkinson, 1980.) Below are some of the questionable communication tactics that I have either witnessed in person or have been told about by reliable sources:

> Taking credit for ideas developed by others (sometimes by outright plagiarism, more commonly by superiors' affixing their names as authors to work done by subordinates).
>
> Pretending to be objective and helpful in raising questions about someone else's proposal, when the real motive is to put that person in a bad light with the boss.
>
> Assigning problems to a committee that has been secretly stacked to assure the support of foregone conclusions.

Doctoring information in a report to make a manager, or a unit, look better than the facts justify (see the disturbing article "Performance Lies Are Hazardous to Organizational Health" [Perry and Barney, 1981]).

Withholding information someone else needs to complete an assignment.

Staging what appears to be participative decision making, when in reality the decision has already been made.

Threatening retaliation against another manager if he or she refuses to grant a concession.

Privately slipping derogatory information (whether true or not) to a higher-up, to undermine the position of another manager.

Using "loaded" agenda, as well as "slanted" minutes, to gain unobtrusive control over the outcome of meetings.

You are free to extend the list *ad nauseam*. The important thing to remember is that dirty tactics are a logical consequence of the faulty assumption that all conflicts of interest are based upon incompatible goals. A few political struggles may indeed be waged over irreconcilable differences, but many—probably the great majority—arise out of goals that are not incompatible. The supposed incompatibilities, as Filley shows, "are frequently *perceived rather than real*" (1975, p. 4).

TAMING THE TIGER OF CORPORATE POLITICS: BASIC PREMISES AND AN AXIOM

Do dirty tricks pay off? Obviously they do on some occasions. But both published and unpublished accounts of business practices supply persuasive evidence that a high proportion of unethical individuals are exposed and that many of their companies suffer a variety of disasters. A safe conclusion seems to be this: Payoffs, when they occur at all, are generally short-term; losses are long-term. As Kotter (1979) observes: "Few people will want to identify with a manipulator. And... a reputation as a manipulator can completely ruin a manager's career" (p. 48).

How, then, is a manager to deal with political realities? Earlier in the chapter, a list of six premises was offered to demonstrate the inevitability of corporate politics. That list is continued here with a set of premises related to political communication. Thinking carefully—and imaginatively—about these premises can help managers build a foundation for the constructive use of power and political strategies.

Premise 7. Politics actually is a civilized method of handling conflicts, especially those arising from the allocation of limited resources.

Premise 8. Dirty tricks become more likely as organizational members believe (whether correctly or not) either (a) that such tactics pay off, or (b) that their very survival is at stake, leaving no recourse but to fight fire with fire.

Premise 9. Whether or not as a conscious policy, many companies do in fact reward unscrupulous politics; or, at the very least, they fail to reward efforts to maintain high ethical standards.

Premise 10. Any kind of conflict, but especially political conflict, can easily deteriorate into a win-lose struggle.

Premise 11. The greatest danger of a win-lose struggle is that someone has to be a loser. Creating losers usually sows the seeds of hostility which can easily lead to all-out warfare. At best, the losers usually suffer from low morale and reduced desire to perform their jobs effectively.

Premise 12. Even the winners in a win-lose contest sometimes experience unfortunate consequences: They can easily become cocky, they may lose the aid and counsel of the defeated antagonists, and they may stumble into ill-conceived decisions.

From these premises we derive the *win-win axiom: The best solution of corporate political conflict is the creation of conditions that permit all parties to become winners.* How can this be done?

1. Encourage all parties to articulate, vigorously and unambiguously, their most urgent *needs* (to be distinguished from mere *desires*).

2. Then engage in free-wheeling discussion—even debate, when necessary—with the objective of discovering what needs the parties have in common. It is inconceivable that the parties share nothing. (Even the Soviet Union and the Western democracies share the common need to avoid extermination.) This discovery process requires great ingenuity (and patience). In other words, imagination—the sixth hallmark—is absolutely indispensable to the entire process of creating win-win conditions.

3. Differentiate (1) *ends from means* (goals from ways of attaining goals), and (2) *higher-level,* or primary, goals from *lower-level,* or subsidiary, goals. No one should ever be asked to abandon a really vital need (see the tactic called *flexible rigidity* under the bargaining guidelines listed later in the chapter).

Filley is unquestionably correct when he says: "Most conflicts involve disagreements of means rather than ends—'my way' versus 'your way'" (1975, p. 26).

4. Explore opportunities for creating *integrative* solutions, through which each party can obtain what it needs. This again requires a high order of imagination. Integrative solutions are invariably off-beat, containing unexpected combinations of ideas. This exploration stage can reflect politics at its best: searching for trade-offs, while stoutly defending one's vital interests. The search is most likely to be successful when parties can somehow rid themselves of the common fixation upon means over ends (or solutions over needs and objectives). Keep everyone's *needs* at the forefront of consciousness and devote most of your energies to finding ways (means to ends) that will satisfy all these needs.

We can now identify the undesirable outcomes of political conflict:

1. *Win-lose:* One side gets everything, or almost everything; the other side, nothing or very little. This outcome is accepted, at least for a limited period of time.
2. *Lose-lose.* Both sides lose.
   a. *Compromise.* Although both sides lose, each side gets something. This outcome, while not ideal, is sometimes the best that can be achieved.
   b. *Premature concession* (see Pruitt and Lewis, 1977). Both sides, in their eagerness to arrive at a settlement, seize upon a poor solution—one that turns out to be unsatisfactory for all parties.
   c. *Stalemate (withdrawal).* Unable to arrive at a solution acceptable to all, the parties abandon the whole negotiation effort; everyone tacitly agrees to continue living with a bad situation.
   d. *Escalation.* After the parties have been unable to arrive at a solution acceptable to all, the losers—or those who perceive themselves as losers—initiate some hostile action, leading to backlash defensive moves by their antagonists, which provokes the first party into further attacks, and so on. Ultimate result: mutual destruction.

Of these five outcomes, only compromise offers much hope for the future, and compromise is far from ideal. Managers should keep these options constantly in mind as they engage in political maneuvering, doing all in their power to bring about a win-win solution—that is, an imaginative solution.

Filley (1975, pp. 74-75) narrates an interesting episode from real life that illustrates a true win-win outcome, an outcome reflecting an integrative solution in which imagination is applied to discovering a method to satisfy the important needs of all parties.

The president of a small electronics company shared an open office with ten other people:

> All eleven people made a practice of getting coffee from an urn located in the corner of the room and carrying it back to their desks to drink while they worked. The company prospered and the previously tiled floor was covered with an expensive carpet. The president issued an order that no more coffee was to be drunk at the desk.

This order precipitated argument and protest, resulting in "hidden threats about who owned the company and about years of loyal service." Then:

> A consultant who happened to be present ... asked the president what he wanted to achieve by forbidding coffee. He said that he did not want coffee stains on the new rug. Then the consultant asked the ... employees what they wanted ... they replied that they wanted to drink coffee at their desks.

There ensued a period of discussion, equivalent to political bargaining. All parties volunteered ideas, and several alternative solutions were proposed and evaluated. Neither the president nor the employees backed way from their stated objectives. So, instead of arguing over these objectives, both sides engaged in vigorous debate over the various proposals—acceptance of ends, disagreement over means. Finally, a solution emerged from the discussions that satisfied everyone: eleven small thermos canisters were purchased, permitting everyone to "fill at the urn and carry to their desks" (keeping the carpet intact). Observe that there was argument and disagreement, but it was confined to an effort to discover an integrative solution rather than to be victorious in a win-lose contest. This, then, was clean politics.

The Cold-Water Corollary

Observe carefully, in the foregoing episode, that the goals of the contending parties were different, but not incompatible. It was found possible to reconcile the objective of drinking coffee at the desks with the objective of preserving the pristine purity of the rug. But we must face the unpalatable truth that occasions do arise on which it seems impossible to reconcile conflicting goals. A robber's goal is to relieve me of all my money, or as much of it as he can find. My goal is to retain every cent.

If an ambitious vice-president has organized his whole life around an obsessive determination to ascend to the presidency of the firm, and if the incumbent president (many years away from retirement) is equally determined to keep her job, there is probably no realistic chance that an integrative solution can be found. Either the parties will settle down to a stalemate (unlikely in the case of the obsessed vice-president), or one of them will leave the company—almost certainly as the outcome of a long-drawn-out battle, with each party lining up allies and inventing new ways of outsmarting the other. In fact, both parties may end up having to leave the company, if the damage has been so great that neither can function successfully.

What all this implies is a corollary of the win-win axiom. I call it the cold-water corollary: *If it is true that either the objectives or the bedrock values of the contending parties are incompatible, then a win-win solution is probably impossible.*

Having accepted the corollary, however, we should base our communication tactics up to the last possible moment upon the assumption of compatibility. Completely irreconcilable objectives—if we ascend the ladder of more and more distant goals far enough—are almost surely a rarity in human affairs. Recall that, even in the most desperate crises, imaginative persuaders have been able to discover integrative solutions that have been accepted by the most fanatic of hostage-takers (in Iran, at airports, in banks, and so on). Invoking the cold-water corollary, then, should be an extremely rare last resort.

We conclude this discussion of politics—constructive, integrative politics—with some guidelines. You will find them on the following pages, arranged in outline format.[3]

Remember that we are discussing informal, day-to-day interactions. We are not attempting to deal with the highly specialized and complex problems associated with formal negotiations, as in union-management collective bargaining. Of course, many basic principles apply across the board to all kinds of situations; but the specific applications to collective bargaining are so unique that they constitute a separate discipline.

Also keep in mind that in the present context, the term *bargaining* and *negotiating* will be used synonymously, as will the terms *advocacy* and *persuasion*.

Exhibit 7.1 will set the stage for the more detailed guidelines to

---

[3]Readers interested in book-length accounts of corporate politics should consult: Dalton (1959), an early classic; Pettigrew (1973), on political tactics in one company; Jay (1974), on Machiavelli and corporate politics; Maccoby (1976), on gamesmanship; and Greeley (1979), on the Vatican. Briefer case histories are to be found in: Kotter (1977, 1979); Peters (1978, 1979); Miles (1980, chap. 6); Pfeffer (1981); and Frost, Mitchell, & Nord (1982).

EXHIBIT 7.1 Managerial Power

Part 1: Analysis of the Manager's Power Potential

A. What resources do I possess or have control over (in greater or lesser degree)?
   1. Nature of the resources
      a. Material, or tangible
         Allocation; scheduling; assignment of equipment, job duties, promotions, salaries, space, budgets, and the like
      b. Nonmaterial, or intangible
         Human understanding, empathy, emotional support, commendation, recognition, friendship, affection, and so on
         Expertise (professional, technical, scientific, and so on)
         Specialized information ("inside dope," knowledge related to job, company, customers, marketplace, competitors, and the like)
         Access to information sources (knowledge of the literature, knowledge of whom to contact for what, and so on)
         Formal authority (legitimacy) relative to specified others
         Time
   2. Quality of the resources
      a. Value to others (in specified situations)
         How critical, how strategic, are the resources?
         How central are they (do they affect many people or operations, or only a few)?
         (*Note:* To what degree are others *aware* of this value?)
      b. Scarcity (relative)
         How limited are the resources? (No scarcity means no power.)
   3. Degree of dependency
      a. How dependent are others upon me? Can they find a substitute?
      b. How dependent am I upon others? Can I find a substitute?
B. How are these resources relevant to interpersonal relationships?
   1. What is my personal network (see Exhibit 7.2), both official (formal) and unofficial (informal): friends, informants, rivals, supporters, opponents, mentors, protégés, counselors, and so on?
   2. What is my past history of favors given or received? What obligations have been created, by me and by others (see Kotter, 1979)?

Part 2: Modes for Using Power

What modes are available to me, as an individual manager or as a member of a coalition?

A. Modes independent of direct, purposeful, verbal communication with specified target ("ecological control," "environmental manipulation")
   1. Modes perceived by target as rewarding
      Justified, earned, fair
      Unjustified, unearned, unfair
   2. Modes perceived by target as punishing
      Justified, earned, fair
      Unjustified, unearned, unfair
   3. Examples of modes which can be either rewarding or punishing:
      Adjustments in pay
      Changes in work schedules
      Changes in physical setting
      Changes in responsibility
      Promotions, demotions
      Changes in task assignments
      Changes in proximity to boss

EXHIBIT 7.1 Managerial Power (continued)

B. Modes depending primarily upon direct, purposeful, communication with target
  1. Basically unilateral influence ("pressure")
     a. Inducement: promises, ingratiation, flattery, bribery
     b. Coercion: threats, intimidation, "high pressure," repetition
     c. Simple request, factual explanation, instructions, orders accepted as legitimate by target: these may require bolstering derived from recognized position, authority, or expertise; from sense of obligation for past favors; or from loyalty to company or altruism
  2. Basically bilateral influence (open confrontation, two-way influence)
     d. "Multiple advocacy," persuasion, debate, discussion (see "Guidelines for Using Advocacy/Persuasion")
     e. Bargaining, negotiating (give and take); may be either formal and structured or informal and unstructured (see "Guidelines for Using Informal Bargaining/Negotiating")
  3. Basically multilateral influence
     f. Collaborative discussion: equalized power, trust and security, sharing of all relevant information (no secrets or hidden agenda)
        An Ideal!
C. Modeling mode (depending upon both verbal and nonverbal behaviors)
   Influencing by example; includes impact of total behavioral repertoire, as perceived by target—manager is a living demonstration
   An Ideal!

---

follow. The first part of the exhibit, "Analysis of the Manager's Power Potential," lays the groundwork for all that follows. The second part, "Modes for Using Power," summarizes what are believed to be the most important options a manager must consider when he or she confronts a situation requiring the deliberate use of power tactics. In this second part of Exhibit 7.1, take special note of the six modes (under Part 2-B) that depend primarily upon direct, purposeful communication.

GUIDELINES FOR USING ADVOCACY/PERSUASION

The following guidelines may be used in those situations in which a manager is initiating and/or defending a major proposal to superiors, peers, or subordinates—each representing, of course, a different level of power relative to the manager. The other party will be called the *persuadee*. For possible persuadees, see Exhibit 7.2, later in the chapter.

1. Make a careful analysis of the degrees and kinds of power available to the manager and to the persuadee (see Exhibit 7.1).
2. Build the presentation upon the fact that a persuadee will accept a new proposal only if, *as he or she perceives it*, the proposal satisfies all five of the following criteria:

a. It meets at least one of these conditions: (1) it satisfies an important personal (or organizational) need; (2) it fulfills a salient desire; (3) it will rectify an existing weakness or deficiency (personal or organizational).
b. It is congruent with personal and organizational values, convictions, ethical/moral standards, and so on.
c. It is workable, practical.
d. Its strengths outweigh the objections to it.
e. No better alternative appears to be available.

3. Do a mental credibility audit: how good is your credibility with this persuadee, on this topic, in this situation? (See Chapter 5.)

4. Consider whether political or power-related factors might be operating to obstruct—or to enhance—your chances for success. If so, what, if anything, can you do about such factors? (Explore the possibility of using third parties; also, think about the effects of any coalitions or cliques, and so on.)

5. Find out if the persuadee has taken a public stand on this proposal—hence, whether he or she feels committed in the eyes of others. If so, does this help your cause, or hurt it?

6. Try to get agreement (as early as possible) on a few basic premises. These can represent overarching goals or values that you and the persuadee share, and from which you can build your case. Often these premises can be fundamental criteria (specifications, standards). If you and the persuadee can find no common ground on premises, persuasion will almost never be possible.

7. Emphasize throughout the discussion a climate of agreement. Proceed, usually, from the less controversial to the more controversial (or "sensitive"), not the other way around. Keep ultimate goals constantly in the foreground.

8. Encourage a two-way dialogue; avoid a monologue. This means that you should not only permit but invite the persuadee to speak out about his or her ideas, reservations, questions, objections, and so on. The more you know about what the persuadee is thinking, the better your chances of demonstrating that your proposal meets his or her criteria. (If such a demonstration is literally impossible, then no persuasion is possible.)

9. Apply the principles of sensitivity (especially receptiveness and responsiveness) discussed in Chapter 6. Be aware of the factors (including choice of words) that may trigger needless defensiveness.

10. Avoid the temptation to "make debate points" just for the sake of showing up the persuadee's deficient arguments. Ignore what appear to be totally untenable arguments and try to get the discussion back to those points (especially the objectives) that you both agree on. If the

persuadee indicates that these untenable arguments are really major considerations, then present your side—but not in a manner suggesting that you win and he or she loses.

11. State points of disagreement candidly, albeit with understanding of how the other person feels. Do not sweep disagreements under the rug. But evaluate the arguments, not the person making them.

12. Avoid behavior that unnecessarily induces deadlocks, such as (a) sweeping generalizations and dogmatic pronouncements; (b) unsupported assertions, when supporting evidence or logic is expected, and (c) simplistic, either-or analyses.

13. Although showing that you are firmly convinced of your position, keep your mind open to the possibility that you may not be the Possessor of Final Truth. Give a fair hearing to ideas raised by the persuadee.

14. As a consequence of Item 13, be ready to modify your original proposal—even rather substantially—if the discussion indicates that a new, integrative proposal is preferable.

15. Never downgrade the importance of cogent logic and hard evidence. Persuasion obtained on the grounds of whims, fancies, and nonrational impulses is not only unethical but risky.

GUIDELINES FOR USING INFORMAL BARGAINING/NEGOTIATING

In a bargaining situation, the other party may be another manager, a superior, or some person—or group—outside the formal corporate structure. Specifically omitted from these guidelines are the special problems associated with bargaining between management and employees. (However, many principles mentioned here are also applicable to that situation.) For a graphic representation of various kinds of parties with whom you might find yourself in a bargaining relationship, see all the nonsubordinate positions in Exhibit 7.2 near the end of this chapter.

1. Don't enter into a bargaining episode without first having clearly determined (and, if you are part of an alliance or coalition, without having group consensus on) what your BATNA is. This is the term coined by Fisher and Ury (1981) to denote your *Best Alternative to a Negotiated Agreement:*

> The reason you negotiate is to produce something better than the results you can obtain without negotiating. What are those results? What is that alternative? What is your BATNA...? *That* is the standard against which any proposed agreement should be measured. That is the only standard

which can protect you both from accepting terms that are too unfavorable and from rejecting terms it would be in your best interest to accept. (Fisher & Ury, 1981, p. 104).

Fisher and Ury make this important point: "People think of negotiating power as being determined by resources like wealth, political connections, physical strength, friends. . . . In fact, the relative negotiating power of two parties depends primarily upon how attractive to each is the option of not reaching agreement" (1981, p. 106).

2. Focus upon objectives, both your own and those of the other party. Postpone evaluation of specific solutions until all parties have had an opportunity to identify and to give vigorous expression to their needs. In general, stress ends over means. (But this does not imply for a moment that you should surrender to the dangerous philosophy "the end justifies any means"!)

3. Noting the discussion of sensitivity in Chapter 6, find ways of making it clear that you honestly can appreciate (even though you may not agree with) the other party's basic goals—as well as his or her fears (even ones you regard as illogical).

4. Defend you own vital interests—your needs and objectives—with all the logical and emotional resources at your command (you will be using persuasion/advocacy here). But, when it comes to considering specific means for achieving your objectives, keep your mind open to all possibilities for arriving at imaginative, "integrative" solutions. This is the strategy that Pruitt and Lewis (1977) appropriately call *flexible rigidity*—being flexible on means, but rigid on ends (ends are, after all, your irreducible needs—to surrender on these would be unacceptable).

5. Avoid laying down ultimatums. Do everything possible to keep the negotiations going. One valuable device is to welcome the opportunity for taking recesses, during which both parties can reassess the situation and their options.

6. Do not assume that 100 percent complete disclosure of all your ideas will be helpful. If it seems likely that two parties subscribe to diametrically opposed ethical values (or philosophical or religious views), then disclosure of these values can make further interaction almost impossible. As Pruitt and Lewis (1977, p. 171) observe, "It can lead to a sense of shock and outrage about the other bargainer's perspectives. This is likely to . . . preclude the development or acceptance of an integrative option, even where an objective analysis would reveal considerable logrolling potential."

7. Do not be so eager for peace and harmony that you settle prematurely upon the first viable solution that presents itself. It may be a poor choice for you—and perhaps for the other party as well. Many bargaining sessions eventuate in harmony and agreement, but only because the parties rush to judgment without thoroughly exploring all

the possibilities. (Again, think of your BATNA. The absence of agreement is preferable to a bad agreement.)

8. Be on the alert for give-and-take opportunities that allow you to make concessions on issues of relatively minor importance to you, but of major importance to the other party.

9. Also be on the alert for opportunities to go up the ladder of needs and objectives until you find one or more that both you and the other party can accept (for example, the shared need to keep the company going).

10. Avoid the temptation to slip into win-lose gamesmanship moves, such as inflation of demands (asking for more than you expect to get just so that you can appear to be making concessions when you accept something less), bluffs, threats of reprisal, concealment of crucial evidence, and the like.

11. When the other party really commands much more power or has many more resources than you, search for all the ways in which he or she may still be dependent upon you. These you can state firmly, but without rancor and without appearing to brandish a weapon. Basically, in a lopsided power relationship in which you are in the lower position, you need to employ the techniques of persuasion—especially those based upon shared values and objectives (see the advocacy/persuasion guide-others as they do with their immediate subordinates.

12. Explicitly invite the other party to engage in a serious exploration for innovative (integrative) solutions, which may have a higher payoff for him or her than would first appear to be the case.

THE REALITY OF THE MANAGER'S INTERPERSONAL RELATIONS

Whether persuading, bargaining, explaining, or just passing the time of day, the typical manager interacts with a host of different individuals. It is easy to accept the stereotypical view of the manager reporting to one or more superiors and presiding over a cadre of subordinates. But this is a severely restricted version of reality. As a number of survey studies have shown (see, for example, the summary in Mintzberg, 1973), most managers spend at least as much time communicating with peers and others as they do with their immediate subordinates.

Any manager concerned about improving his or her communication effectiveness must, in the final analysis, think not in terms of an over-all bundle of skills, but rather in terms of this question: With what individuals do I communicate, and how effective am I (both as message sender and listener) in each of these relationships? What is really required, then, is a person-by-person and situation-by-situation analysis of the communication exigencies associated with each interpersonal relationship. This sounds like a tall order, and indeed—if the manager is serious about improving his or her communication—it is a tall order. Fortunately, we carry out much of this analysis rather painlessly, almost automatically, from hour to hour. However, a systematic self-improvement effort calls for more.

What is recommended, then, is that you picture yourself as the constantly moving hub of a network of communication relationships. Examine Exhibit 7.2, a graphic illustration of this idea. Of course, this "relational map"—for a hypothetical manager designated by the large letter M in the center—is a gross oversimplification. Most managers experience many more interpersonal relationships than the twenty or so indicated by the numbered lines in Exhibit 7.2. But at least the map will suggest the wide variety of communication contacts existing for a typical manager in a typical work setting.

If the graph is to be useful, we must first translate the symbols. Every line in the exhibit (whether single or double) represents some sort of significant communication. The double lines refer to direct reporting (superior-subordinate) relationships, as in a chain of command. All lines are numbered, for convenient reference.

The various boxes designate persons with whom the manager communicates, or who communicate with each other. The meanings of the symbols within the boxes are as follows:

Ex   A high level executive.

B   The manager's immediate superior—that is, boss.

SRa   A manager at a higher level than M's, but not M's superior.

SRb   Another manager at a higher level, but in this case a manager to whom M reports in a matrix structure.

(The four-person matrix, arranged in a diamond-shaped pattern, is diagramed at the lower right corner of the graph, with **Ex** shown as the person in charge, and with **M**'s regular boss **B** and **M**'s "second boss" **SRb** shown as persons having supervisory responsibilities over **M**.)[4]

st   Any staff specialist with whom **M** communicates such as a person in public relations, personnel, or purchasing.

O   Any individual outside the company with whom **M**

---

[4]It is not possible to include a discussion of the matrix organization here. An excellent book-length treatment of the subject is offered by Kingdon (1973). Brief reviews concentrating on the importance of negotiation and persuasion skills can be found in Sayles (1976) and Lawrence, Kolodny, and Davis (1977). The political, bargaining, and advocacy skills discussed in this chapter are indispensible for managers operating in matrix structures.

The Reality of the Manager's Interpersonal Relations **125**

EXHIBIT 7.2   The Manager's Relational Map

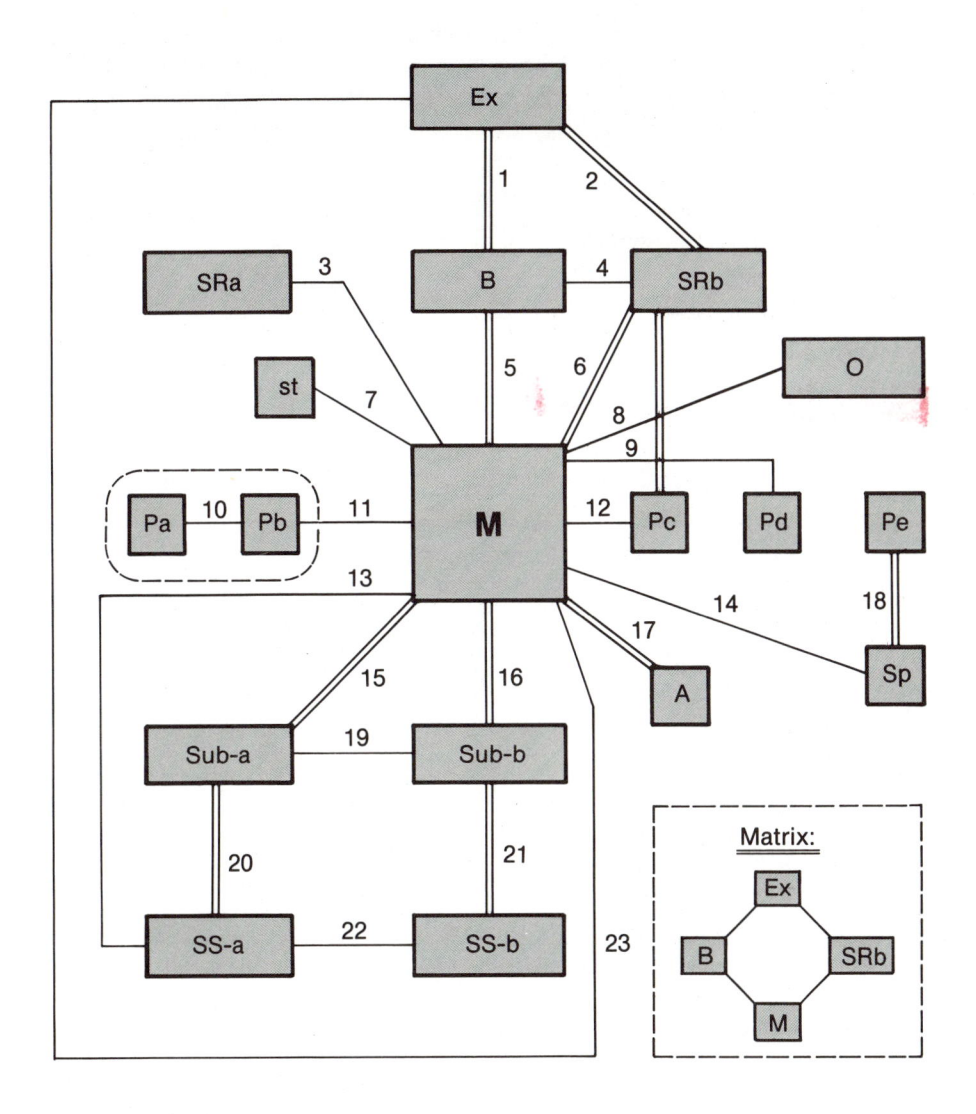

126 *Idealism Confronts Reality: People, Power, and Politics*

communicates on matters related either directly or indirectly to company business.

Pa, Pb, Pc, Pd, Pe Other managers at about the same hierarchical level as **M**—in other words, **M**'s peers. (Lines 9, 11, and 12 indicate that **M** communicates directly with only **Pb, Pc,** and **Pd**; Line 10, that **M** communicates indirectly—through **Pb**—with **Pa. M** does not communicate at all with **Pe.**)

Sub-a and **Sub-b** Managerial or supervisory subordinates reporting directly to **M** (hence double lines 15 and 16).

A Any assistant (such as a secretary or a formally designated assistant) reporting directly to **M**).

SS-a and **SS-b** Subordinates of **M**'s subordinates: **SS-a** reports to **Sub-a; SS-b,** to **Sub-b** (double lines 20, 21).

SP The subordinate of peer manager **Pe** (double line 18).

Note certain relationships:

Line 14 Line 14 shows that **M** communicates directly with **Sp,** but not at all with **Sp**'s boss (**Pe**)—an arrangement that could mean lots of trouble.

Line 22 Line 22 shows that **SS-a** and **SS-b** communicate directly with each other, although they report to different bosses.

Line 23 Line 23 shows that **M** has a direct communication channel to the top executive, **Ex,** bypassing **M**'s boss (**B**), as well as **SR-b.**

Line 13 Similarly, **M** maintains direct communication with a subordinate's subordinate (**SS-a**)—a case of "downward bypassing."

Broken-line oval, enclosing Pa *and* Pb The oval designates an alliance or coalition—for political purposes—between peer managers **Pa** and **Pb** (such a coalition might or might not include subordinates of **Pa** and **Pb,** not shown on the map).

You can conjure up all kinds of images and stories suggested by the boxes and lines in Exhibit 7.2. The surface has barely been scratched. But this has no doubt been enough to illustrate the basic concept of a manager's interpersonal relationships.

It is suggested that you quickly rough out, with pencil and paper, your own relational map. Then start thinking about each of the communication relationships depicted. When you do this, you should be posing such questions as the following:

- What is the interpersonal climate of each relationship? That is, is it formal or informal, friendly or cool, and so on?
- What are the power dependencies (two-way) between myself and each communicant? For what does the other person depend upon me, and for what do I depend upon him or her? What resources (both tangible and intangible) does each of us possess? (See Exhibit 7.1, Part 1.)
- What topics are easy to discuss with this other person? Why? What topics are difficult (or even impossible) to discuss? Why? Can anything be done to change this state of affairs? Are there third-party intermediaries who might be useful?
- What favors has each of us done for the other? Are there any resulting obligations? With what consequences? Do such obligations work in my favor, or not?
- How about our reciprocal credibilities? On specified topics, how credible am I with this other person; how credible is the other person with me? If I have credibility problems, what can I do to alleviate them (including the introduction of evidence or the possible use of third parties respected by the other person)?
- How about our communication history? Have we had any serious disagreements, even quarrels? With what consequences?
- On what topics (including concepts, even words) is it most likely that, because of different backgrounds, we will misunderstand each other? What common ground do we share?
- What is the likelihood that either of us will feel threatened and hence resort to defensive communication? What can I do or say to reduce the level of threat? (See Chapter 6.)
- When will the other party be in a state of mental readiness to discuss a given topic with me? What are the best choices of time, place, setting, media, and modalities (such as face-to-face meeting, telephone conversation, formal memo, or informal note)?
- Which of the three basic modes of using power, and which of the six communication modes of influence, are probably most appropriate with the other party, in this situation? (See Part 2 of Exhibit 7.1.)

One theme of this chapter has been that managers will always have difficulty in trying to apply the ideals of good communication in the turbulent, unpredictable, politics-ridden corporate world. But there has been a second theme: With imagination (the sixth hallmark), ingenious managers will find ways of being effective communicators without compromising ethical standards.

References

Bacharach, Samuel B., and Edward J. Lawler. *Power and Politics in Organizations.* San Francisco: Jossey-Bass, 1980.

Barnard, Chester I. *The Functions of the Executive.* Cambridge, MA: Harvard University Press, 1938; 30th anniversary ed., 1968.

Bennis, Warren. "An Interview with Warren Bennis." *Organizational Dynamics* 2, no. 3 (Winter 1974): 50-66.

Dalton, Melville. *Men Who Manage.* New York: Wiley, 1959.

Deutsch, Arnold R. *The Human Resources Revolution.* New York: McGraw-Hill, 1979.

Filley, Alan C. *Interpersonal Conflict Resolution.* Glenview, IL: Scott, Foresman, 1975.

Fisher, Roger, and William Ury. *Getting to Yes: Negotiating Without Giving In.* Boston: Houghton Mifflin, 1981.

Frost, Peter J., Vance F. Mitchell, and Walter R. Nord, eds. *Organizational Reality—Reports from the Firing Line,* 2nd ed. Glenview, IL: Scott, Foresman, 1982.

Greeley, Andrew M. *The Making of the Popes 1978.* Kansas City, MO: Andrews and McMeel, 1979.

Jay, Antony. *Management and Machiavelli: An Inquiry into the Politics of Corporate Life.* New York: Bantam Books, 1974.

Kingdon, Donald R. *Matrix Organization: Managing Information Technologies.* London: Tavistock, 1973.

Kipnis, David. *The Powerholders.* Chicago: University of Chicago Press, 1976.

Kipnis, David, Stuart M. Schmidt, and I. Wilkinson. "Intraorganizational Influence Tactics: Explorations in Getting One's Way." *Journal of Applied Psychology* 65 (1980): 440-52.

Kotter, John P. "Power, Dependence, and Effective Management." *Harvard Business Review* 55, no. 4 (July-August 1977): 125-36.

Kotter, John P. *Power in Management.* New York: Amacom, 1979.

Lakoff, George, and Mark Johnson. *Metaphors We Live By.* Chicago: University of Chicago Press, 1980.

Lawrence, Paul R., Harvey F. Kolodny, and Stanley M. Davis. "The Human Side of the Matrix." *Organizational Dynamics,* 6, no. 1 (Summer 1977): 43-61.

Lee, James A. *The Gold and the Garbage in Management Theories and Prescriptions.* Athens: Ohio University Press, 1980.

McCaskey, Michael B. "The Hidden Messages Managers Send." *Harvard Business Review* 57, no. 6 (November-December 1979): 135-48.

Maccoby, Michael. *The Gamesman.* New York: Simon and Schuster, 1976.

March, James G., and Herbert A. Simon. *Organizations.* New York: Wiley, 1958.

Miles, Robert H. *Macro Organizational Behavior.* Glenview, IL: Scott, Foresman, 1980.

Mintzberg, Henry. *The Nature of Managerial Work.* New York: Harper & Row, 1973.

Nord, Walter R., and Douglas E. Durand. "What's Wrong with the Human Resources Approach to Management?" *Organizational Dynamics* 6, no. 3 (Winter 1978): 13-25.

Ortony, Andrew, ed. *Metaphor and Thought.* New York: Cambridge University Press, 1979.

Perrow, Charles. *Complex Organizations: A Critical Essay.* 2nd ed. Glenview, IL: Scott, Foresman, 1979.

Perrow, Charles. "Organization Theory in a Society of Organizations." Transcript of a lecture, circulated by the Red Feather Institute for Advanced Studies in Sociology. Center for Policy Study, State University of New York at Stony Brook, February 1980.

Perry, Lee T., and Jay B. Barney. "Performance Lies Are Hazardous to Organizational Health." *Organizational Dynamics* 9, no. 3 (Winter 1981): 68-80.

Peters, Thomas J. "Symbols, Patterns, and Settings: An Optimistic Case for Getting Things Done." *Organizational Dynamics* 7, no. 2 (Autumn 1978): 2-23.

Peters, Thomas J. "Leadership: Sad Facts and Silver Linings." *Harvard Business Review* 57, no. 6 (November-December 1979): 164-72.

Pettigrew, Andrew M. *The Politics of Organizational Decision-Making.* London: Tavistock, 1973.

Pfeffer, Jeffrey. *Power in Organizations.* Boston: Pitman, 1981.

Pfeffer, Jeffrey, and Gerald R. Salancik. "Organization Design: The Case for a Coalitional Model of Organizations." *Organizational Dynamics* 6, no. 2 (Autumn 1977): 15-29.

Pruitt, Dean G., and Steven A. Lewis. "The Psychology of Integrative Bargaining." In Daniel Druckman, ed., *Negotiations.* Beverly Hills, CA: Sage, 1977, pp. 161-92.

Sayles, Leonard R. "Matrix Management: The Structure with a Future." *Organizational Dynamics* 5, no. 2 (Autumn 1976): 2-17.

Schein, Virginia E. "Individual Power and Political Behaviors in Organizations: An Inadequately Explored Reality." *Academy of Management Review* 2 (1977): 64-72.

Weick, Karl E. *The Social Psychology of Organizing,* 2nd ed. Reading, MA: Addison-Wesley, 1979.

Wise, David. *The Politics of Lying.* New York: Random House, 1973.

Zaleznik, Abraham, and Manfred F. R. Kets de Vries. *Power and the Corporate Mind.* Boston: Houghton Mifflin, 1975.

CHAPTER 8

The Big Picture: Communication and Human Resources Management

> Because superior human resources create the most central, basic, and powerful strategic competitive advantage possible, human resources management should receive top priority. . . . A group of loyal, productive employees is an organization's most effective competitive weapon.

These assertions appeared in a recent article in the *Harvard Business Review* (Skinner, 1981, pp. 112-14). Most practicing managers, as well as almost all academic authorities on management, would no doubt agree. And yet, as the author of this article reluctantly reported, the available evidence suggests that only a minority of U.S. companies have experienced notable success in utilizing their human resources as those resources could be utilized.

As stated early in Chapter 1, this book frankly subscribes to the central premises underlying the approach that has come to be called "human resources" management. This does not imply endorsement of every contention carrying the "human resources" label. One thing it does imply is commitment to the human resources axiom, which can be stated as follows: The most effective organization is the one that is most successful in using the full range of talents, skills, and creativity—that is, human resources—represented by all the people belonging to the organization.

To call this principle an axiom is a fair statement of the case. What manager could possibly argue against it? Who would contend that a company should deliberately neglect any fraction of the human resources available to it? The issue is not, therefore, whether to utilize human resources, but how.

Members of the classical school of management—such as Taylor (the father of scientific management) and Weber (the theorist who first analyzed bureaucracy)—were convinced that their prescriptions would enable large organizations to make effective and efficient use of human resources (even though they never used the term). In like manner, the devotees of the human relations school (commonly associated with Harvard University and the historic research studies at the Hawthorne plant of Western Electric) argued that if managers would treat their employees as human beings and make them feel important as members of the team, organizations would enjoy high morale, which would in turn lead to high productivity. An oversimplified expression of the human relations approach would probably be: "A happy worker is a productive worker." We now know, after years of collecting data from empirical studies, that this conclusion is untenable—even though no one denies the importance of having a satisfied work force. An employee who is downright miserable will almost certainly be a poor producer, but highly satisfied workers can also be poor producers.

A brief guidebook like this one is hardly the proper forum for examining the arguments and counterarguments supporting and opposing the various schools of management theory. For present purposes, we should be aware that both the traditional and the human relations approaches have come under fire from a host of critics, especially since the early 1960s. Scientific management and classical bureaucracy have been charged with being rigid, ignoring the human needs of employees, failing to utilize the abilities and ideas of lower-level members, and discouraging creativity. The human relations model has been accused of being manipulative, superficial, and not very good at getting the work done.[1]

And so, in recent years, the phrase *human resources*—admittedly used in different senses by different authors—has come to symbolize a variety of "new design" approaches. These designs typically incorporate several basic changes: (a) changes in the structure of the organization (for example, matrix, Theory Z, "adhocracy"); (b) changes in the structuring of jobs (for example, job enrichment à la Herzberg); and especially (c) changes relating to the use of participative decision making (PDM). Raymond E. Miles was perhaps the first to insist that human resources management differs sharply from human relations manage-

---

[1]For a comprehensive and highly readable review of all these—and more—attacks upon both the traditional and the human relations schools of thought, see Perrow (1979).

ment, a position that he expounded persuasively in a famous *Harvard Business Review* article published in 1965.

The distinction between the two is of particular significance for managerial communication. The reason is that participation in decision making is at the very heart of human resources management, and participation is a communication device: when people participate, they talk with each other.

In his 1965 article, as in all his subsequent writings, Miles distinguishes between authentic participation and cosmetic participation. In the human relations model, the objective of "participation" is to make subordinates feel better, and thereby to induce "compliance with managerial authority" (Miles, 1965, p. 150). Therefore, this kind of participation remains at a superficial level (Shall we place the water cooler over here or over there?). It is a subtle form of persuasion rather than a gut-level exchange of views on matters of major significance. The human resources model, on the other hand, starts from the premise that all—or virtually all—subordinates have unique and important contributions; they have expertise, experience, know-how. They are mature adults with "creative ability and the capacity for responsible, self-directed, self-controlled behavior" (Miles, 1965, p. 150). We can easily recognize, in these assumptions, the well-known postulates of McGregor's Theory Y (McGregor, 1960), as well as those of Herzberg's "motivation" factors in job enrichment (Herzberg, 1968).

HUMAN RESOURCES MANAGEMENT AND RISKY COMMUNICATION

For managerial communicators, the kind of participation required by the human resources model means that managers must be willing to share important information with all participating decision makers—whether subordinates, peers, or their own bosses. Sharing information—especially information that has been traditionally regarded as the exclusive property of management—involves a certain degree of risk, of course. But good decision making can only be informed decision making.

Hence, human resources management implies *open communication, built upon reciprocal trust* (not blind trust, but rather what Barnes [1981] calls *tentative trust*). In the management context, it is helpful to remember that openness is a two-way affair. That is, openness applies both to telling and to listening. Moreover, it applies (potentially) to any of the communicants shown on the relational map (Exhibit 7.2) in the last chapter: subordinates, superiors, peers, and others. Openness in telling refers to candor and honesty, willingness to disclose relevant information, frankness in expressing one's ideas and feelings. Openness in listening refers to receptiveness to divergent views, ability to handle criticism, and recognition of the usefulness of a speaker's ideas regardless of his or her status. An open communication climate implies, therefore, that people are actively encouraged to express dissent, to explore pros and cons, to engage in vigorous debate when significant issues are at stake.

All this, even in the best of times, is indeed risky. But a number of companies have earned the reputation of making remarkable progress toward the idea of an open communication climate—to mention a few of them, Hewlett-Packard, Honeywell, IBM, Intel, Sherwin-Williams, TRW, and Xerox. For example, Intel (one of the well-known occupants of California's Silicon Valley) makes it a policy to encourage all employees to "challenge senior executives as equals" in decision-making sessions. A news story reported that James Jarrett, Intel's manager of corporate communication, described company meetings as occasions where "people are expected to bring things out. Just being polite is a disservice.... Anyone giving a presentation can expect intense questioning.... This atmosphere pervades all meetings, and debate enemies may really be the best of friends" *(IABC News,* March 1981, p. 3).

A cautionary note: Communicating openly does not mean disclosing everything to everybody! Some delicate negotiations (such as those producing the United States Constitution) would collapse were the participants compelled to defend their every utterance in public. Warren Bennis has written eloquently, from the vantage point of his own experience as a college administrator, of the damage that can be done by adhering to a rigid position of complete disclosure (see the essay "Meet Me in Macy's Window" in Bennis, 1976, pp. 114–24).

Roger D'Aprix, a communication manager at Xerox for many years, makes a powerful case for openness; he insists that only three kinds of information should be closely guarded: (a) "proprietary product information," (b) critical aspects of "business strategy," and (c) information that would violate "another employee's right to privacy" (D'Aprix, 1977, pp. 121–22). The burden of proof, as D'Aprix urges, should remain with those who would withhold, rather than with those who would disclose, information.

BEWARE THE MOTIVATION MYTH: BACK TO THE BASIC COMMUNICATION QUIZ

Human resources management, in the final analysis, rests upon an all-encompassing assumption, the assumption of "abundance rather than scarcity in the area of human capabilities, which in turn indicates that the manager's role is not so much one of controlling organization members as it is of facilitating their performance" (Miles, 1975, p. 42).

Many managers, however, seem to use a double standard in applying this assumption. Large-scale survey findings, summarized by Miles (1975, pp. 45-49), indicate that managers rate themselves high on such attributes as "responsibility," "judgment," and "initiative," while at the same time rating their subordinates as relatively low on these same attributes. Thus, we encounter the widespread feeling that subordinates are not capable—or at least not yet ready—for assuming major responsibilities, or for participating in important decision making. In other words, as Miles points out, too many managers expect their bosses to apply the tenets of human resource management, while hesitating to apply these tenets to their subordinates.

For example, I have found in my own experience a disturbing number of practicing managers who agree with questionnaire items like the following:

- If left to do as they pleased, most employees would "goof off" most of the time.
- Relatively few employees have the expertise or breadth of view required to participate meaningfully in significant decisions.

But when I have substituted the word *managers* for the word *employees* in these items, I have consistently obtained 100-percent rejection of these assertions! (Interestingly enough, employees frequently agree that "most *managers* will goof off if given the opportunity.")

Assumptions like these are bound to have an impact upon the ways a manager communicates with subordinates. They encourage managers to maintain constant surveillance over employees, to ignore employees' suggestions, to resist sharing information, and to use orders—or high-pressure persuasion—in an effort to "motivate" subordinates.

Let's look at the age-old question: "How can we motivate our people to do high-quality work?" A fundamental problem arises in the very wording of the question. It asks how *we* can motivate *other people*. But the fact of the matter is that no human being can literally motivate another. People can only motivate themselves. All that we, especially as managers, can do is to help create an environment in which people have the opportunity to motivate themselves. (This is not to deny the unfortunate fact that, until all the world's drudgery can be turned over to computer-driven robots, many jobs and job environments will provide little opportunity for any normal human being to become motivated.)

As Peter Drucker has recently maintained, we should stop asking ourselves how we can motivate people and inquire instead how we can avoid quenching motivation. "We now know that the human being is a learning machine, and the problem is not to motivate people but to keep from turning them off. The quickest way to quench motivation is not to allow people to do what they've been trained to do" (Drucker, 1982, p.

62). As an example, Drucker proposes that we modify the work environment of nurses, who spend 80 percent of their time on paperwork instead of on nursing.

Perhaps the most serious communication blunder committed by well-meaning managers in their efforts to motivate employees is to assume that inspirational appeals (whether in speeches, in essays in house organs, or in cartoons on bulletin boards) will really be significantly effective. This assumption I call the *motivation myth*. But it's based on faulty psychology. If anything, as many surveys have shown, pep talks from management frequently have a boomerang effect—employees are likely to regard such efforts as condescending, if not downright insulting. (See the discussion of the human dignity axiom in Chapter 6.)

Does all this mean that managerial communication can have no relevance whatever to employee motivation? Not at all. The chief contributions managerial communication can make toward the goal of activating employee motivation are these:

1. Management can provide information (accurate, candid information) showing that there really is a connection between quality of work effort and attainment of desired rewards. Keep in mind that only the employee can determine what is truly rewarding, whether it be higher pay, better working hours, more insurance coverage, profit sharing, recognition and commendation from the boss, promotion, or satisfaction from utilizing his or her talents to accomplish a task worth doing for its own sake. Regrettably, as Kerr (1982) showed conclusively in a much-reprinted essay, organizations commonly commit the "folly of rewarding A, while hoping for B." In academe, this can take the form of making public pronouncements about the primacy of good teaching, while in fact basing tenure and promotions on the number of column inches of published research. If there is no consistent connection between performance and rewards (or if the supposed rewards are not perceived as rewards at all by those getting them), then no amount of communication will salvage the situation.[2]

2. Management can encourage participative setting of high performance goals. Researchers have long recognized that, up to a reasonable limit, the higher one sets goals, the more one achieves. Latham and Locke (1979) summarized the findings from ten representative field studies, ranging over a wide variety of jobs and skills.* Their over-all conclusion: "goal setting significantly increases the level of production— by an average of 19 percent in the studies summarized in this review—

---

[2]Probably the most dominant contemporary psychological theory of work motivation is the *Valence-Instrumentality-Expectancy* (or *VIE*) theory. If you are interested in expanding your horizons in this area, an excellent comprehensive exposition will be found in Campbell and Pritchard (1976).

*Excerpted, by permission of the publisher, from "Goal Setting—A Motivational Technique that Works" by Gary P. Latham and Edwin A. Locke, *Organizational Dynamics*, Autumn 1979, pp. 68 and 74. Copyright © 1979 by AMACOM, a division of American Management Associations, New York. All rights reserved.

and reduces absenteeism and injuries" (p. 68). This outcome occurred, as the authors note, whether supervisors set the goals unilaterally or whether the entire work group participated in the process.

However, in a study conducted in a forest products company employing workers with low educational backgrounds, the authors came up with results they described as "startling." They had expected that these employees would perform better when goals were set unilaterally by supervisors. They had predicted that such workers would be either unable or unwilling to set high productivity standards for themselves. And they had reasoned that, even if the workers did set high standards, they would fail to achieve them without close supervision. The results were exactly contrary to these predictions: "The uneducated crews... who participated in goal setting, set significantly higher goals and attained them more often than did those whose goals were assigned by the supervisor" (Latham & Locke, 1979, p. 74).

Note that these findings directly refute Item 7 in the Basic Communication Quiz (Chapter 1):

A ⓓ ?   7. If you let employees set their own productivity standards, most of the time they will set standards that are too low in terms of efficiency and profitability for the firm.

The study described above was not an isolated case. The assumptions about human beings proposed in human resources management theory have held up in much (although not all) real-life research.

3. *Management can provide rapid and reliable feedback about job performance.* Little need be added here regarding the crucial importance of feedback; the topic was covered earlier. In this context, we can think of such devices as performance reviews, computer-assisted reports of work outcomes, quality circles, and—perhaps most important of all—daily, informal conversations between employee and supervisor and among employees. Of this much we can be certain: One of the surest ways of squelching motivation is to deprive people (including managers themselves) of access to information regarding the results of their performance, or to supply such information only in sporadic, delayed, or confusing fashion. Can feedback showing that a worker has performed *poorly* have a depressing effect upon motivation and future performance? Yes, it can; no doubt about it. But this fact argues only that managers should create a supportive environment in which they can thrash out such problems candidly, rather than suppress bad news. (Eventually, the truth will come out, anyway.)

4. This is the biggest point of all: *Management communication can create a supportive emotional climate by fulfilling the ten communication responsibilities listed in Chapter 4 and by striving for candid, open, and sensitive communication* (see especially Chapters 5 and 6, with par-

ticular attention to credibility and sensitivity). A field survey study, done by Penley and Hawkins (1981), offers strong evidence that the total communication climate can affect employee motivation. The researchers surveyed 354 employees of a financial institution in the Southwest to learn employees' perceptions of supervisory and managerial communication. Their conclusions indicated that the following communication practices exerted important influence on employee motivation:

a. Supervisors' willingness to listen, to accept feedback, and to give feedback (see feedback receptiveness and feedback responsiveness in Chapter 6).
b. Supervisors' willingness to give deserved praise (the best form of praise, as we know, focuses upon deeds and results, not upon the person or the personality of the employee).
c. Creativity in using a wide variety of channels and media to transmit information about goals, benefits, and the reward system (see Chapter 4 for lists of media and methods).
d. Provision of detailed information regarding opportunities for advancing up the career ladder.

Probably no single task a manager undertakes is more critical in its effect upon employee motivation than the performance appraisal interview. Hence, Exhibit 8.1 provides a number of suggestions for conducting such an interview.

Now look at Items 5 and 6 in the Basic Communication Quiz:

A(D)? 5. Generally speaking, the best managers are those who can (a) *initiate* good ideas or decisions and then (b) *sell* them to their colleagues—superiors, peers, or subordinates.

Certainly this assertion is not totally false. The trouble is that it is a half-truth. Although persuasive skill is unquestionably useful to any manager, the item—as worded—reflects a one-way-influence conception of management. It sets up the manager as fountainhead of all good ideas, as well as salesperson *par excellence.* The best managers should be not only good persuaders but also good listeners and good catalysts.

A(D)? 6. The most effective managerial communicators are able to take into account a universal law of human nature: People generally resist change.

In my experience, this item elicits close to 100-percent agreement from all kinds of respondents. It's easy to agree with because it's so plausible. However, it serves to perpetuate one of the most destructive

EXHIBIT 8.1 Tips for Managers: Conducting Performance Appraisals

There is a large specialized literature, including a number of books, dealing with performance appraisal. What follows is highly selective, designed to include only the highlights. For a quick overview, two sources are strongly recommended: *Organizational Dynamics*—the entire Winter 1981 issue—and the book by Robert G. Johnson (1979).

Be aware of prior conditions that should exist (ideally).
1. "A supportive organizational climate that fosters a problem-oriented approach to a wide variety of issues" (Sashkin, 1981, p. 46).
2. Day-by-day interaction between superior and subordinate, especially focusing upon informal coaching and feedback—"Thus the appraisal interview is merely a review of issues that have already been discussed" (Beer, 1981, p. 32).
3. Company policies that do not require mechanical adherence to a standardized, rating-scale form and that do not require approval by a manager's boss of such a form before the employee sees it. (Such policies force the manager into rigidity and especially into a position in which he or she feels compelled to argue defensively, thus fostering an adversarial relationship in the interview.)

Make advance preparations.
1. Hold a "pre-interview interview" in which manager and subordinate meet to come to mutual understanding on the purposes and procedures to be followed and on the kind of outcomes (in terms of future actions) to be expected. Manager can stress that a counseling, problem-solving approach is to be adopted.
2. *Subordinate* should be encouraged to write out his or her own evaluation of performance, with reference to objectives and established criteria. (During the interview itself, however, both the manager and the subordinate might well work from a blank evaluation form, if a form is required, or from no documents whatever.)
3. *Superior* should do careful analysis (with or without filling out forms) to clarify in his or her mind the following: objectives and criteria to be agreed upon; a limited number of problems or weaknesses in the subordinate's performance that need to be addressed; strengths to be encouraged and to serve as foundations for future progress; consideration of which factors are and which are not under the control of either the subordinate or the manager; exploration of possible corrective or developmental steps to be taken.

Separate evaluation from development.
Evaluation requires the manager to be a judge; development, a helper. The roles of judge and helper are incompatible. One is directive and potentially adversarial; the other is nondirective, cooperative—essentially problem-solving. If company policy requires that these two functions be accomplished in the same interview, make an agreement with subordinates that development and counseling will come first, with any required formal evaluation at the end (Beer, 1981, p. 33).

If salary or promotion is to be discussed, schedule these topics for a separate, follow-up interview. Encourage subordinates to evaluate you, their manager, especially in terms of how you might have helped, or might help in the future, to provide assistance and support.

Seek to identify and to secure agreement on these basic premises:
1. Goals or objectives—preferably those that have emerged from earlier conferences, representing consensus.
2. Nature of the evidence to be used to estimate accomplishment (quantitative measures? examples of tasks completed? public recognition received? reports and documents? cost figures?).
3. Criteria by which performance is to be evaluated (quantity or quality of productivity? human relations? innovativeness?). Notice the value here of using "critical incidents" describing actual cases of superior and of inadequate performance.

Set some guidelines for communication during the interview.
1. Emphasize *description* of specific, *observable* instances of behavior rather than evaluative remarks, especially those applied to broad, vague *personality* attributes. For example:

EXHIBIT 8.1 Tips for Managers: (continued)

"Three of your old customers cancelled their orders last month, and all of them claimed that they had not been told certain vital facts." (instead of: "You must be losing your grip.")
2. Do more listening than talking. Johnson (1979) recommends that the manager talk no more than 10 percent of the total time. This means you must try to get the subordinate to initiate major points and to take the lead in assessing his or her own performance.
3. To accomplish this objective, use nondirective techniques (especially in the first half to two-thirds of the interview):
Emphasize open-ended questions (instead of closed questions, especially yes-no questions). For example:
"How do you feel about the way things have gone in your department the past six months?" (instead of: "What caused you to run over budget again?" or: "Do you have incompetent staff people?")
Ask for two-way feedback to compare reactions and identify possible misunderstandings. For example:
"When I said that a few minutes ago, here's what I was driving at.... Did I mislead you?" "I get the impression that you feel maybe I've let you down. I hadn't thought of it that way, but I can see now that you might have come to this conclusion. Tell me more." "Let me see if I get the drift here...."
Use neutral encouragements, inviting the subordinate to give more details, more examples, more explanation:
"Uh-huh." "I see." "Hmmmm... tell me more."
"That's interesting... and what happened after that?"
Use paraphrases, summaries, "mirror responses" indicating that you understand and empathize (but not necessarily that you agree). For example:
"You really felt that you were taking all the heat, didn't you?" "You must have thought this office really goofed." "You're wondering whether this assignment put you between a rock and a hard place, right?"
Become directive only after the subordinate has had ample opportunity to volunteer evaluations and suggestions for future actions, but has failed to do so. For example:
"Has it occurred to you that you might schedule a weekly meeting of your people..." "I wonder whether you could profit from taking this evening course we've just started up; it's called 'Living with the Computer.'"
Make outcomes and next steps clear. Do this cooperatively, inviting the subordinate to suggest what should be done after the interview is over. Think of steps in terms of what the subordinate can do something about, then of what you can do to assist the subordinate. If there are deficiencies or mistakes that require immediate correction, make this need very explicit and get agreement on exactly what will be done.

In general, follow a strategy of limited objectives.
As Johnson has observed: "If an appraisal form were made extensive enough, we would all fail.... We must limit ourselves to the possible" (1979, p. 18). Narrow down the objectives to a small number of points, those that really *must* be addressed.
In general, encourage the subordinate to write down lists of consequences for each action that may be taken in the future; be sure to include both good and not so good (or disastrous!) consequences that may be expected. (See Latham, Cummings, & Mitchell, 1981, p. 21.)
In general, strive for a problem-solving climate (as opposed to judging or blaming or game playing).
In general, try to escape from lots of paper work (rating scales and so on). Especially avoid formal evaluation sheets that focus on global, intangible traits like "attitude," "initiative," "loyalty," and the like.
Finally, don't get so nondirective that you fail to express your own views!

fallacies plaguing not only managers but just about everybody in positions of leadership. And yet it is easily refuted. Do most people resist change when the change consists of a raise in pay?

What is it about change that we resist, then? Is it the change itself? Not at all. In fact, change is essential for sustaining life. Without constant changes—billions of them every hour—we would be dead. And without change, we experience suffocating boredom. What we resist is *threat,* including the threat posed by uncertainty. Managers should therefore stop worrying about employees' resistance to change and start worrying instead about whether they will perceive threat in the proposed change.

Be aware of a hidden assumption related to this topic: that employees resist change because they are incapable of understanding the complexities of the situation. In other words, the assumption is that only managers initiate changes, while subordinates react to them (usually negatively). When exposed to the light of day, this kind of elitist thinking reveals its own fallibility. What managers need to do is to find out why any proposed change may be perceived as a threat. Keep in mind that many proposed changes are indeed threatening. When this is the case, managers must communicate the facts with unflinching candor. Also keep in mind that when people participate in generating changes, they seldom resist those changes.

We are back to participation (PDM), with all its risks and all its promises. This is understandable, since participation lies at the very core of human resources communication.

APPLYING HUMAN RESOURCES PRINCIPLES TO MANAGERIAL COMMUNICATION SYSTEMS

Responsible critics have leveled attacks against various features of human resources management, including McGregor's (1960) Theory Y formulations (which comprise much of the philosophical underpinning of the entire human resources rationale). The design of this book prohibits a rehearsal of the charges and rebuttals. Readers wishing to get a quick overview of the issues and arguments can consult articles in such journals as *Harvard Business Review, Organizational Dynamics,* and *Academy of Management Review.* For thoughtful attacks I especially recommend Lee (1971) and Nord and Durand (1978). For balanced consideration of both pros and cons, see Barnes (1981), Kanter (1982), and Skinner (1981). For strong defenses, see Blake and Mouton (1982), Lawler (1978), Miles and Rosenberg (1982), and Pasmore (1982).

A common theme voiced by both the critics and the defenders has been that verbal support of the human resources approach is almost universal, whereas actual application to real life is debatable. For managers "to argue effectively against Modern Human Resource Management," wrote Lee "would be tantamount to shooting Smokey Bear for sport" (1971, p. 20). And, more recently, Skinner concluded that "Human resources management seems to be mostly good intentions and whistling in the dark or averting unionization" (1981, p. 107).

No claim is made that a preponderance of U.S. companies have successfully installed human resources management in all its aspects. But we cannot ignore the evidence that an impressive number of them have indeed put it into practice, with favorable results. Some of this evidence is summarized in Exhibit 8.2.

Further, a detailed case history of the installation of totally new methods applying human resources management at the Richmond (Kentucky) plant of Sherwin-Williams is provided by Poza and Markus (1980). A cardinal provision in the plant charter at Richmond asserts this premise: "We will operate . . . in a manner that demonstrates good communications, respect for people, honesty, openness, and a responsiveness to realistic ideas and suggestions from both the plant personnel and the community . . ." (p. 11). Statistical measures reported by Poza and Markus indicate phenomenal accomplishments—productivity 30 percent higher than in other plants, absenteeism 63 percent lower, a 94-percent quality rating (compared with a 75-percent all-plant average), a 25-percent reduction in "failure costs," and so on. The inescapable conclusion is that, idealistic as human resources management sounds, its principles *can* be applied in everyday practice.

Of course, we must keep things in perspective. Refer once more to Exhibit 5.2 (Chapter 5), which depicted the numerous "forces and constraints exerting impact upon a manager's behavior." All these forces can create formidable problems for any manager attempting to apply human resources principles. For example, think of the pool of human beings available for employment, and the particular individuals with whom a manager must work. Even Maslow (1965) conceded that his methods would not work with certain people (p. 184). And it was McGregor

---

EXHIBIT 8.2 **New-Design Plants**

Lawler (1978) estimated that—as of 1978—no fewer than fifty U.S. organizations had developed and successfully operated "new-design" plants ("new design" being an approximate synonym for human resources management and involving the restructuring of technology, of jobs, and of the authority hierarchy). Some of the companies he named included: Cummins Engine, Dana Corporation, General Foods, General Motors, H. J. Heinz, Mead Corporation, PPG Industries, Procter & Gamble, Rockwell, Sherwin-Williams, and TRW. In earlier pages we have already identified others, such as Hewlett-Packard, Honeywell, IBM, and Intel.

himself who declared that a manager "cannot have confidence in a genuinely incompetent, or a dishonest, or a neurotically hostile subordinate" and that "some personalities are simply incompatible" (1960, pp. 141-42). Similarly, we know that human resources communication methods are easier to apply in some technologies than in others, and in some organizational structures than in others. See especially Mintzberg (1981). And there is Kanter's (1979) convincing argument that many managers are almost forced into "oppressive" rather than "productive" uses of power by the fact that they occupy low-power, dead-end jobs.

Finally, disturbing though it may be, we should reflect upon the dark possibility suggested a few years ago by E. J. Webb, when he wrote: "How robust will the humanistic values inherent in participative management be when organizations struggle for their very survival? Can we preserve openness and concern for others when people are fighting to maintain their private empires, departments or even their jobs?" (Quoted by Nord, 1976, p. 709.)

Even without assuming such a gloomy future, we should be aware of the fact that dozens of contingencies can influence the kinds and degrees of PDM that are feasible in any given situation: not only personality attributes, but cultural norms, the degree of control individuals exercise over their work, and many more (for a long list of these, see Kanter, 1982).

Having said all this, however, we come back to the fundamental fact that the kind of communication recommended here—that described by the six hallmarks of excellence and based upon the concepts of human resources management—is demonstrably applicable to the real corporate world: "There is no longer a meaningful debate in the United States about the applicability of the human resources approach to management" (Miles & Rosenberg, 1982, p. 41).

The chapter ends with two instruments relating to the corporate domain of managerial communication. The first is Exhibit 8.3, the Managerial Communication Climate Questionnaire. Its forty items represent criteria, drawn from the human resources point of view, for evaluating the perceived communication climate of a firm. It is for diagnostic and training purposes only. No claim is made that it is a precise scientific measuring instrument. Because climate reflects basic assumptions and value premises—such as those of McGregor's Theory X or Theory Y—its impact far outweighs that of any specific behavioral act or any media event. By examining the ratings that you (or others) assign to each item, you can begin to identify strengths and weaknesses in the corporate communication climate.

The second instrument, Exhibit 8.4, represents an overview of most components of the total corporate communication system (climate is just one of these components). It is arranged in outline, checklist format and

EXHIBIT 8.3 Managerial-Communication Climate Questionnaire

KEY: AAT The statement is almost always true
UT   The statement is usually true
UF   The statement is usually false
AAF The statement is almost always false

To indicate your response, draw a circle around *one* of the four symbols preceding each item.

AAT	UT	UF	AAF	1.	It's easy to find out what's going on; there are few secrets around here.
AAT	UT	UF	AAF	2.	People feel free to say what's on their minds when they're talking to their bosses.
AAT	UT	UF	AAF	3.	You can count on the truth and accuracy of what company management says about such matters as profits and losses, long-range plans, and impending changes of policy.
AAT	UT	UF	AAF	4.	Other managers at my level in the company are people with whom I can easily and frankly discuss mutual problems.
AAT	UT	UF	AAF	5.	My superiors keep me informed on what's expected of me—of what I must do to get ahead.
AAT	UT	UF	AAF	6.	Managers encourage subordinates to come up with new ideas, and they protect them when they stick their necks out by making suggestions.
AAT	UT	UF	AAF	7.	Company statements are oted for their clarity and freedom from bureaucratic prose.
AAT	UT	UF	AAF	8.	Management treats everyone with respect—as mature adults rather than as children.
AAT	UT	UF	AAF	9.	Management is candid in disclosing bad news; the rule is, "We tell it like it is."
AAT	UT	UF	AAF	10.	Performance appraisals are conducted in such a way that the subordinate knows where he or she stands and participates in setting his or her own goals for continued progress.
AAT	UT	UF	AAF	11.	The underlying assumption in the company is that just about everybody has good ideas, and that these ideas should contribute to all major decision making.
AAT	UT	UF	AAF	12.	When you send messages to higher management, you get a prompt and honest response.
AAT	UT	UF	AAF	13.	When you see a crisis building up, it's easy to alert higher management about it.
AAT	UT	UF	AAF	14.	Generally speaking, I receive all the information I need to perform my job effectively.
AAT	UT	UF	AAF	15.	People representing different departments and different specialties have ample opportunity to consult with each other.

EXHIBIT 8.3 Managerial-Communication Questionnaire (continued)

AAT	UT	UF	AAF	16.	This company plays down status differences between superiors and subordinates.
AAT	UT	UF	AAF	17.	Managers at all levels are encouraged to be their own bosses—hence, to take risks.
AAT	UT	UF	AAF	18.	In this company, we stress that managers should act more as counselors and helpers than as order givers and watchmen.
AAT	UT	UF	AAF	19.	Although I am treated with consideration at all times, am "stretched" to achieve high performance goals.
AAT	UT	UF	AAF	20.	The general spirit around here is: "We're all in this boat together, and we sink or swim together" (rather than: "The way to get ahead is to outmaneuver your rivals").
AAT	UT	UF	AAF	21.	I find it relatively easy to get feedback from my subordinates about their problems, feelings, and accomplishments.
AAT	UT	UF	AAF	22.	I find it relatively easy to get feedback from my superiors when I send messages asking for information, answers to questions, and so on.
AAT	UT	UF	AAF	23.	Our publications, for both managers and employees, are known for candor, for completeness, and for providing "gutsy" information.
AAT	UT	UF	AAF	24.	Higher management is willing to listen to criticism; it approaches new ideas with an open mind, even when these ideas imply criticism.
AAT	UT	UF	AAF	25.	The company provides a systematic and safe means for anyone to raise questions or criticisms; and questions are answered promptly, fully, and accurately by appropriate line managers.
AAT	UT	UF	AAF	26.	When someone offers an idea or makes a proposal in decision-making conferences, my approach is: "Let's see why this might be a good idea" (rather than: "What's wrong with it").
AAT	UT	UF	AAF	27.	In this company, people feel that managers are sincerely interested in their welfare and progress.
AAT	UT	UF	AAF	28.	If I am making a major proposal to higher management, I know that I'll get a fair hearing; I'll be subjected to searching questions, but I can talk back without fear of the consequences.
AAT	UT	UF	AAF	29.	When one of my own subordinates is making a major proposal, I give him or her a fair hearing; I subject the proposal to searching questions, but I encourage the subordinate to talk back without fear of the consequences.

EXHIBIT 8.3 Managerial-Communication Questionnaire (continued)

AAT UT UF AAF 30. When important news about the company is announced, both managers and employees hear it first before it's released to the general public.

Below are a number of communication practices that many people find objectionable, or at least ineffective. Indicate whether you believe each is a problem in your company.

AAT UT UF AAF 31. It's wise to protect oneself by keeping "just-in-case" files of past actions and decisions.

AAT UT UF AAF 32. The rule here is: If you make a mistake, you hear about it immediately. But if you do a good job, you can wait until hell freezes over before you get any recognition.

AAT UT UF AAF 33. Higher management acts as if it has all the answers: "Don't worry, we know best."

AAT UT UF AAF 34. Management's idea of getting high productivity is to put on high-pressure sloganeering campaigns, the basic message being "Work harder!"

AAT UT UF AAF 35. The safest rule to follow around here is: Be careful what you say to whom.

AAT UT UF AAF 36. When important developments occur in the company, we generally hear about them first from sources outside the company (such as friends, neighbors, newspapers).

AAT UT UF AAF 37. Management is constantly springing surprises on us.

AAT UT UF AAF 38. This is a cold, impersonal company, where the rule book is supreme and management "manages by memo."

AAT UT UF AAF 39. The best way for a manager to get ahead here is to cultivate the right people: "It's not what you know, but who you know."

AAT UT UF AAF 40. When I think of top management, I think of the Great Stone Face: No matter how loudly you yell or how often you ask questions, all you get is silence.

Potential problems can be identified by false answers (UF, AAF) on Items 1 through 30; and true answers (AAT, UT) on Items 31 through 40.

---

should be especially useful in evaluating the company's over-all communication effort and in planning communication policies.[3]

---

[3] It should be obvious that human resources management requires consummate skill in the handling of all kinds of small-group communication situations, whether for information exchange, problem solving, brainstorming, or decision making. Space limitations preclude the inclusion here of a separate section or chapter devoted to this important topic. The reader is referred to the excellent treatment of small-group communication in Robert Hopper, *Between You and Me: The Professional's Guide to Interpersonal Communication* (Glenview, IL: Scott, Foresman and Company, 1984).

146   *The Big Picture: Communication and Human Resources Management*

EXHIBIT 8.4   The Internal Corporate Communication System: A Checklist

I. Information adequacy (To what degree does each organizational member have the information he or she needs to function effectively on the job?)
   A. General dissemination of information
      1. Recipients
         a. Does information reach the right people? Are some who need the information skipped?
         b. If dissemination is severely restricted, is there a defensible rationale for this?
      2. Channels (see also A-7 and A-8)
         a. Are the shortest, most direct channels utilized (instead of those with relays)?
         b. Are the channels appropriate (perceived as conforming to accepted norms)?
         c. Is transmission of information speedy (or subject to needless delays)?
      3. Redundancy (planned)
         a. For high-priority messages, where understanding and retention are crucial, is there the right amount of redundancy (neither too little nor too much)? (Redundancy may exist within a single message, in various forms of repetition or restatement; between messages, when a message is repeated at different times and places; or between media, when the same message is repeated in different ways via different media).
         b. Is the redundancy presented in such a manner that receivers are not insulted, irritated, or fatigued? (Does communication show imagination, ingenuity?)
      4. Consistency
         a. Are different messages congruent with each other (or are there inconsistencies, even contradictions, between one message and another)?
         b. Are the messages disseminated internally congruent with those disseminated externally (such as those contained in mass media advertising, TV interviews with executives, and the like)?
      5. Density (avoidance of either overload or underload)
         a. Is too much (or too little) information being transmitted to given recipients in too short (or too long) a time to permit comprehension and assimilation of messages?
      6. Selectivity (distinction between higher- and lower-priority messages or ideas)
         a. Are the higher-priority messages (or components within messages) presented with greater use of attention-getting techniques and emphasis? (If all messages, or all ideas, are presented at the same level of emphasis—either high or low—the more crucial will be drowned out.)
      7. Media and settings (see also A-2 and A-8)
         a. Are the media chosen for specified messages the most appropriate (in terms of audio or visual requirements, ease of access, privacy, and so on)?
         b. Is proper attention given to the benefits of informal media and informal settings (versus over-reliance upon the formal)? Examples: informal or handwritten memos, luncheon conversations, hallway or rest-area conversations, off-site meetings, and the like.
         c. Are media and settings chosen to enhance official authority (when this is called for), or to deemphasize status differences (when this is desirable)?
      8. Authentication versus the grapevine and informal networks (see also A-2 and A-7)
         a. Is thought given to which messages, on which occasions, need to be authenticated (guaranteed to be officially authorized)—and which ones should be left in an unofficial, off-the-record, tentative state—"trial balloons," for the time being?
         b. Is there recognition of the many values to be found in rumors, gossip, and the grapevine in general, and of the advantages in encouraging the formation of informal networks, all as important parts of the total dissemination system?
      9. Built-in feedback loops
         a. Are formally approved channels provided to secure feedback to management-

EXHIBIT 8.4   The Internal Corporate Communication System: (continued)

        generated messages? (Examples: sensing sessions, question-and-answer plans, "speak-up" programs, informal small-group meetings, formal attitude and readership surveys, and the like.)
      b. Are there systematized requirements to ensure rapid, accurate, and candid responses to feedback received (from the highest-level managers possible)?
- B. General message effectiveness
  1. Adaptation to recipients' special needs and desires for information
      a. Are recipients likely to perceive the message as relevant to their interests and welfare? (If not, either modify the message to show such relevance, or don't send the message.)
      b. Are messages adapted to recipients' background of education, training, experience, and so on? (Beware especially of falling into the conveyor-belt fallacy.)
      c. Are messages timed appropriately? (Do communicators take into account recipients' probable state of mind, mood, receptivity, immediate setting, and so on, as well as how recipients will perceive this message in relation to certain prior messages?)
      d. Are messages consistently accurate, and are they as complete as circumstances will allow? (Or is unwelcome news swept under the rug, sensitive issues downplayed, and so on?)
  2. Application of universal communication principles
      a. Is ingenuity applied to finding attention-getting and interesting methods for expressing ideas (without being condescending or insulting the recipients' intelligence)?
      b. Is skillful use made of such devices as graphics, pictures, analogies, metaphors, and the like?
  3. Consideration of problems especially associated with the organizational setting
      a. Do mass media messages avoid falling into the "Pollyanna trap"? (This refers to the common tendency to publish nothing but laudatory material and good news, frequently with a preponderance of attention given to relatively trivial topics, such as "the three Bs"—baseball, bowling, and babies.)
      b. Do messages avoid the risk of being perceived as sermons, full of platitudes, from superior beings (management) to peasants (employees)? (Think twice before singing exuberant hymns of praise to free enterprise, for example.)
      c. When controversial issues are being discussed, is forthright advocacy tempered with fairness toward other views (or is it all one-sided, completely ignoring the existence of other opinions)?
      d. Do mass media messages seem to focus on overworked stereotypes (such as the brilliant decisions of top management, the "bottom line," or the like)?
      e. Within the bounds of authentication (see A-8), is corporate prose free from two extremes: bureaucratese or gobbledygook (excessive legalism, formality, complexity, jargon) on the one hand and an oversimplified, condescending, "shirtsleeve" style on the other? (Recommended reading: Mitchell, 1979; Whyte, 1952.)
- C. Effectiveness in articulating major objectives and central themes of the company
  Do all the communication efforts and events interact to keep attention focused on the big picture, on long-term goals, on basic company philosophy? (Or do efforts seem to take a scattergun approach, in which communication resembles a mere collection of miscellaneous activities?) To what extent is there careful, centralized planning behind the total system?
- D. Consideration of communication costs (what does it cost to disseminate information compared with the indirect costs incurred if the information is not disseminated?)
  1. Human costs (time and energy, stress, and so on)
  2. Material costs (money, materials, equipment, and so on)
  3. Time costs (how much time is required?)

EXHIBIT 8.4 The Internal Corporate Communication System: (continued)

II. Structural dimensions of corporate communication
   A. Subject matter of downward-directed communication (topics found in surveys to be important to employees and middle and lower levels of management)
      Note: Topics are listed below in descending rank-order, according to preferences reported by several thousand employees in *ICA Audit* surveys (conducted under sponsorship of the International Communication Association; see Porter, 1979).
      1. How organizational decisions (affecting my job) are made
      2. Promotion and advancement opportunities and policies
      3. How my job-related problems are being handled
      4. How my performance is being judged
      5. Specific problems being faced by top management
      6. Major organizational policies
      7. Important new developments (such as products, services)
      8. Mistakes, failures of the organization
      9. Pay, benefits: scales, policies, and so on
      10. How well I am doing in my job
      11. How my job relates to total corporate operations
      12. How technological changes affect, or will affect, me
      13. Instructions on job duties
   B. Subject matter of upward-directed communication (topics believed to be important, both for sender-subordinates and for receiver-managers)
      Note: Since these topics come from a variety of sources, they are listed in random order. Those at the top of the list are not necessarily more important than the others.
      1. Evaluation of the performance of immediate superiors
      2. Reports of problems encountered on the job
      3. Reports of accomplishments, tasks completed, and so on
      4. Questions about corporate policies, procedures, and the like
      5. Early warning signals of impending crises
      6. Expressions of dissent on policies, procedures, decisions
      7. Bad news—reports of failures, breakdowns, mistakes, and so on
      8. Suggestions to improve effectiveness or efficiency of operations (applicable to one's own job or to the company as a whole)
      9. Issues regarding budget allocations, policies, criteria
      10. Proposals for major innovations (applicable to job, unit, or whole company)
      11. Complaints about alleged management errors, bad decisions, questionable ethics, and so on (This is internal whistle-blowing. It can lead to external whistle-blowing.)
   C. Communication taking place outside the vertical hierarchical structure
      1. To what extent are task forces, project teams, and matrix structures utilized? (Are they effective?)
      2. To what extent do managers find it easy to interact with other managers (peers, those occupying positions outside the division, and so on)? What arrangements—if any—facilitate coordination among units—including staff meetings and the like?
      3. To what extent do managers find it feasible to establish, or to join, informal networks crossing both functional and status lines (horizontal and diagonal channels)? To what extent do managers obtain valuable information through these informal networks?
      4. How easy is it for a lower-level manager to bypass a superior to contact a higher-level manager?
      5. Is there free exchange of ideas between managers and important outside sources of information and new ideas? (Or does the company retreat behind barricades into a state of insulation from the outside world?)

EXHIBIT 8.4 The Internal Corporate Communication System: (continued)

  6. To what extent do alliances, cliques, and coalitions take shape? With constructive or destructive effects?
  D. Use of channels and special methods for facilitating upward communication (including ombudsmen)
     These channels may be either formal (official) or informal (unofficial). For a list of possibilities, see Chapter 4
III. Organizational memory and information-retrieval systems
  A. Records and accessibility to historical events
     Without accessible records of important past events ("memory"), there can be no continuity of policies or procedures. Note the importance of informal memories supplied by old-timers and knowledgeable staff members.
  B. Information-retrieval systems
     These include filing systems, computerized access systems, and company libraries.
IV. Attitudinal characteristics of the communication system as a whole—climate. (*Note:* for detailed items, see the climate questionnaire (Exhibit 8.3) preceeding this checklist.
  A. Perceptions (primarily by subordinates) of managers as human beings
     See the six hallmarks: self-worth, integrity, wisdom, credibility, sensitivity, imagination.
  B. Perceptions of attitudes underlying the entire corporate communication system—primary requisites
     1. Supportiveness and openness (see especially Chapter 5, on sensitivity)
     2. Encouragement of participative decision making
     3. Credibility (of the corporation as a whole, as distinguished from individual managers): remember C-R-I (competence, reliability, good intentions)
     4. Insistence upon maintaining high performance standards
  C. Confidence that the company is performing a valuable social function and is aware of ethical responsibilities

References

Barnes, Louis B. "Managing the Paradox of Organizational Trust." *Harvard Business Review* 59, no. 2 (March–April 1981): 107–16.

Beer, Michael. "Performance Appraisal: Dilemmas and Possibilities." *Organizational Dynamics* 9, no. 3 (Winter 1981): 24–36.

Bennis, Warren. *The Unconscious Conspiracy.* New York: Amacom, 1976.

Blake, Robert R., and Jane S. Mouton. "A Comparative Analysis of Situationism and 9,9 Management by Principle." *Organizational Dynamics* 10, no. 4 (Spring 1982): 20–34.

Campbell, John P., and Robert D. Pritchard. "Motivation Theory in Industrial and Organizational Psychology." In Marvin D. Dunnette, ed., *Handbook of Industrial and Organizational Psychology.* Chicago: Rand McNally, 1976, pp. 63–130.

D'Aprix, Roger M. *The Believable Corporation.* New York: Amacom, 1977.

Drucker, Peter F. "A Conversation with Peter F. Drucker." *Psychology Today,* December 1982, pp. 60–67.

Herzberg, Frederick. "One More Time: How Do You Motivate Employees?" *Harvard Business Review* 46, no. 1 (January-February 1968): 53-62.

Johnson, Robert G. *The Appraisal Interview Guide.* New York: Amacom, 1979.

Kanter, Rosabeth Moss. "Power Failure in Management Circuits." *Harvard Business Review* 57, no. 4 (July-August 1979): 65-75.

Kanter, Rosabeth Moss. "Dilemmas of Managing Participation." *Organizational Dynamics* 11, no. 1 (Summer 1982): 5-27.

Kerr, Steven. "On the Folly of Rewarding A, While Hoping for B." In Peter J. Frost, Vance F. Mitchell, and Walter R. Nord, eds., *Organizational Reality: Reports from the Firing Line*, 2nd ed. Glenview, IL: Scott, Foresman, 1982, pp. 497-512. Originally published in *Academy of Management Journal* 18 (1975): 769-83.

Latham, Gary P., Larry L. Cummings, and Terence R. Mitchell. "Behavioral Strategies to Improve Productivity." *Organizational Dynamics* 9, no. 3 (Winter 1981): 4-23.

Latham, Gary P., and Edwin A. Locke. "Goal Setting—A Motivational Technique That Works." *Organizational Dynamics* 8, no. 2 (Autumn 1979): 68-80.

Lawler, Edward E., III. "The New Plant Revolution." *Organizational Dynamics* 6, no. 3 (Winter 1978): 2-12.

Lee, James A. "Keeping Informed: Behavioral Theory vs. Reality." *Harvard Business Review* 49, no. 2 (March-April 1971): 20-28, 157-59.

McGregor, Douglas M. *The Human Side of Enterprise.* New York: McGraw-Hill, 1960.

Maslow, Abraham. *Eupsychian Management—a Journal.* Homewood, IL: Irwin, 1965.

Miles, Raymond E. "Keeping Informed: Human Relations or Human Resources?" *Harvard Business Review* 43, no. 4 (July-August 1965): 148-63.

Miles, Raymond E. *Theories of Management: Implications for Organizational Behavior and Development.* New York: McGraw-Hill, 1975.

Miles, Raymond E., and Howard R. Rosenberg. "The Human Resources Approach to Management: Second-Generation Issues." *Organizational Dynamics* 10, no. 3 (Winter 1982): 26-41.

Mintzberg, Henry. "Organizational Design: Fashion or Fit?" *Harvard Business Review* 59, no. 1 (January-February 1981): 103-16.

Mitchell, Richard. *Less Than Words Can Say.* Boston: Little, Brown, 1979.

Nord, Walter R., ed. *Concepts and Controversy in Organizational Behavior*, 2nd ed. Glenview, IL: Scott, Foresman, 1976.

Nord, Walter R., and Douglas E. Durand. "What's Wrong with the Human Resources Approach to Management?" *Organizational Dynamics* 6, no. 3 (Winter 1978): 13-25.

Pasmore, William A. "Overcoming the Roadblocks in Work-Restructuring Efforts." *Organizational Dynamics* 10, no. 4 (Spring 1982): 54-67.

Penley, Larry E., and Brian L. Hawkins. "Communicating for Improved Motivation and Performance." In W. K. Fallon, ed., *Effective Communication on the Job.* New York: Amacom, 1981, pp. 120-25.

Perrow, Charles. *Complex Organizations: A Critical Essay,* 2nd ed. Glenview, IL: Scott, Foresman, 1979.

Porter, D. Thomas. "The ICA Communication Audit: 1979." West Lafayette, IN: Department of Communication, Purdue University, 1979.

Poza, Ernesto, and M. Lynn Markus. "Success Story: The Team Approach to Work Restructuring." *Organizational Dynamics* 8, no. 3 (Winter 1980): 2-25.

Sashkin, Marshall. "Appraising Appraisal: Ten Lessons from Research for Practice." *Organizational Dynamics* 9, no. 3 (Winter 1981): 37-50.

Skinner, Wickham. "Big Hat, No Cattle: Managing Human Resources." *Harvard Business Review* 59, no. 5 (September-October 1981): 106-14.

Whyte, William H., Jr. *Is Anybody Listening?* New York: Simon & Schuster, 1952.

INDEX

Absenteeism, 5
Action, program of, 17
Adaptability, 28
Adaptation, 98
"Adhocracy," 131
Advocacy, 117
   guidelines for use of, 119-120
Alliances, 110
Application of new technique, 18
Argyris, Chris, 90
Arterburn, David, 89
Articulation of goals, 54
Assertiveness, 92, 95-96
Assumptions, 14
   correct vs. incorrect, 25
   identification of, 16, 24-26
AT & T Long Lines, 7-8
Attitude, 14
Audience, 43-45
Authoritarian management style, 10-11
Awareness of situation, 89, 91-92

Back-burner fallacy, 26-27
Bargaining, 112, 117
   guidelines for use of, 121-123
Barnard, Chester I., 38, 107
Barnes, Louis B., 25
Basic communication quiz, 2-3, 133-140
BATNA, 121
Bennis, Warren, 107
Brainstorming, 45
Brevity, 40

Case histories, 3-13
Channels of communication, 43
Charisma, 53
Coalitions, 110

Code of ethics, of observer, 66-67
Cold-water corollary, 116-117
Communication
   basic, quick course in, 31-34
   breakdown, 9-10
   deficiencies, causes of, 14
   definitions of, 1, 13-14
   face-to-face, 5
   managerial. *See* Managerial
      communication
   one-way, 35-36
   open lines of, 6-7
   overlap, 33-34
   "package," 11
   quiz for managers, 2-3, 133-140
   roles, 30
   specific skills of, 1
   "underground," 13-14
Compromise, 115
Concern, 88-90
   for others, 88-89
   for self, 89-90
Condescension of, 61-62
Conflict of interest, 112
Conflict resolution, 55
Confrontation meetings, 46
Consciousness raising, 16, 21-22, 97-98
Conveyor-belt fallacy, 30-34
   consequences of, 34-36
Coordinating activities, 55
Corporate Cultures, 29-30
Corporate politics, 108-109, 113-119
   "dirty tricks," 113
Corporate publications, 8-9, 12
Corporate representation, 55-56
Credibility, 63, 71-80
   audit, 79-80
   dimensions of, 73-75
   importance of, 75-80
   low, 77-79

153

Index

D'Aprix, Roger, 58, 133
Deal, Terrence, E., 29, 92
Defensive communication behavior, 4-5
Delegation corollary, 26
Delphi groups, 45
Democracy, industrial, 5
Dependency, and power, 110-113
Deutsch, Arnold R., 105
Dignity, 100
Di Salvo, Vincent, 89
Double interact, 31
Double-loop learning, 90
Drucker, Peter, 134

Employee survey research, 84-85
Employee(s)
  feedback from, 12-14
  perceptions of, 86
Equity, 53
Escalation, 115
Ethical code, of observer, 66-67
Excellence, five hallmarks of, 65, 71, 100
Executive paranoia, 8
Expressiveness, 92, 95-96

Face-to-face communication, 5
Fallacies, 26-37
  back-burner, 26-27
  conveyor-belt, 30-34
    consequences of, 34-36
  quick-fix, 27-28
  visibility, 28-30
Feedback
  continual, 18-19
  defined, 18
  from employees, 12-14
  importance of, 31-32
  receptiveness, 94
  relevancy of, 31-32
  responsiveness, 94
  soliciting and accepting, 35-36
Flesch, Rudolf, 35
Flexible rigidity, 122
Fortune, 36
Fragmentation, 40
Full information disclosure, 7-8

General Motors, Tarrytown, 5-6
Gibb, Jack, 73
Glauser, Michael J., 66
Goals, articulation of, 54

Greeley, Andrew, 109
Gulick, Luther, 39

Haire, Mason, 95
Hallmarks of excellence, 65, 71, 100
Harvard Business Review, 25, 67, 88
Headquarters relocation, 7-8
Hewlett-Packard, 133
High-tech manufacturers, 6-7
Honesty, 61
  in communicating bad news, 6-7
Honeywell, 45, 133
Human dignity axiom, 101
Human function, 54
Human relations, 53
Human resources management, 2
  and communication, 130-149
Human resources utilization, 56

Ideal managerial communicator, 62-63
  basic personality attributes of, 63-64
  developing, 68-69
Idealism vs. reality, 104
Imagination, 104
Industrial democracy, 5
Information dissemination, 55
Innovativeness, 56-57
Insensitivity
  in managerial communication, 83-85
  manifestations of, 82-86
Integrity, 63, 65, 66-67
Intel, 133
Internal corporate communication
  system: a checklist, 146-149
International Business Machines (IBM),
  45, 133

Jarrett, James, 133
Job performance, of subordinates, 55
Johnson, Mark, 105

Kahn, Robert L., 53, 54, 69-71
Kanter, Rosabeth Moss, 68-69
Katz, Daniel, 53, 54, 69-71
Kennedy, Allan A., 29, 92
Kets de Vries, Manfred F. R., 88
Kipnis, David, 110
Kotter, John P., 110

Index

Lakoff, George, 105
Lee, Irving, 34
Lesly, Philip, 38
Levinson, Harvey, 86
Listening, 35-36
Loyalty, 57

Maintenance function, 54
Management
   participatory vs. authoritarian, 10-11
   repressive, 4-5
Manager
   communication responsibilities of, 38-58
      six minimum requirements, 46-47
   interpersonal relationships of, 123-127
   job description of, 39-41
   job profiles of, 41
   oral skills and responsibilities of, 40
   role of, 41
Managerial communication
   climate questionnaire, 142, 143-145
   corporate responsibilities of, 53-57
   domains of, 16, 47-53
   defensive style of, 4-5
   examples of, 3-13
   fallacies of, 26-27. See also Fallacies
   isolation, 35
   personal domain, 47-51
      vs. corporate domain, 48-51
   scope of, 42-47
   with subordinates, 100
   systems, applying human resource principles to, 140-142
Managerial power, 118-119
Managerial role, 41
Manipulation, 13-14
Matrix, 131
McCaskey, Michael B., 105-106
Media, 43
Memoranda, 19-20
   overkill, 19-20
Message-receiving, 42
Metaperception, 88
Metaphors, 105-106
Miles, Raymond E., 131-132
Miles, Robert H., 107
Mintzberg, Henry, 39-40
Misunderstanding
   mutual, 88
   prevention of, 88
Modalities, 45
Motivation
   fear as, 8-9
   myth of, 133-144

National Airlines, 83-84
Negotiation, 117
   guidelines for use of, 121-123
"New-design" plants, 141
Nine-step schedule to self-improvement, 15, 16-19
   consciousness raising, 16, 21-22
   implementation of, 19-21
"Noble Self," 98

One-in-five, 12, 13-14
Open communication, 6-7
Opinion Research Corporation (ORC), 85

Paranoia, executive, 8
Participatory management, 10-11
Perception(s)
   of communication failure, 9-10
   of employees, 86
   of perceptions (metaperception), 87-88
Perceptiveness, 92, 96-101
Performance appraisals, how to conduct, 138-139
Pernow, Charles, 107
Personal domain of managerial communication, 47
   vs. corporate domain, 48-51
Personal style, 22
Perspective, 69-71
Persuasion, 117
   guidelines for use of, 119-121
Peters, T. J., 29
Pfeffer, Jeffrey, 109
POSDCORB, 39, 40, 41
Postman, Neil, 91
Power, managerial, 118-119
Practice, 17-18
Premature concession, 115
Priorities, 29
"Priests," 30
Productivity, 58

Quality circles, 5-6
Quality of work life, 5-6
Question-answer programs, 45
Quick course in basic communication, 31-34
Quick-fix fallacy, 27-28

Index

Ragan, Janine, 84
Ragan Report, 84
Receptiveness, 92, 94-95
  feedback, 94
Reciprocal communication, 95
Reciprocal trust, 132
Responsibilities, communication, 38-58
  checklist of, 54-57
Responsiveness, 92, 94-95
  feedback, 94
"Rhetorical Reflector," 98
RHETSEN scale, 98, 99
Roundtable, 12

Satisfying workplace, 56
Schedule, communication, 19-22
  identifying assumptions, 24-26
  implementation of, 19-21
  raising consciousness, 21-22
Schein, Virginia, 108
Scope of managerial communication, 42-47
"Secrets," 27-28
Seeking feedback, 18-19
Self-awareness, developing, 2-3
Self-fulfilling prophecy, 106
Self-improvement
  misfired attempts at, 22
  nine-step schedule, 15, 16-19
  personalized program of, 16-17
Self-worth, 63, 65, 66
Semantic environment, 91
Senders, message, 73
  vs. receivers, 73-74
Sensing sessions, 12-13
Sensitivity
  of communicator, 82-86
    attributes of, 92-101
  managerial, 88-92
  rhetorical, 98
  training, 17, 82, 86
  triad, 97
"The Six M's of Management," 39
Skills, specific communication, 1
Slogans, 58
Smith, Roger, 95
Sherwin-Williams, 133
"Spies," 30
Split-level, 12
Spokesman, 41

Stalemate, 115
Statement-making, 34-35
Stewart, Rosemary, 41
Stimuli, 32
Stockdale, James B., 66, 67
"Storytellers," 30
"Strategy-making," 41
Subordinates, gauging performance of, 55
Superior-subordinate pairs, 34-35
Supportiveness, 92, 93
  vs. defensiveness, 93-94
  six criteria of, 93-94
  of supervision, 93-94
Survey research, 84-85
Symbols, physical manifestations of, 32-34

Taking stock, 17
Task function, 54
T-groups, 82, 86
Theories, espoused vs. in action, 90
Theory Y, 132
Theory Z, 131
Tips for managers, 138-139
Topic coverage, 29
Transmitting messages, 43-44
Trust, tentative, 25
TRW, 12-14, 133
Two-way feedback, 36, 95

Understanding, 33
  development of, 87-88
"Undiscussability," 90
United States Maritime Commission, 84-85

Valence-Instrumentality Expectance (VIE) theory, 135
Variety, 40
Videotape, ingenious use of, 46
Visibility fallacy, 28-30

Wall Street Journal, 66
Weick, Karl, 106
Westinghouse, 11-12
"Whisperers," 30

Whyte, William H., Jr., 36
Wisdom, 63, 65, 67–68
Wise, David, 111
Women, in business, 39
Workplace improvement, 56
Written communication, 46, 51

Xerox, 133

"Yes-men," 31

"Zero defects," 31